Grammar and Punctuation

Key Stage 2
Scotland P4-P7

Wendy Wren

First published in 1999 by:
Stanley Thornes (Publishers) Ltd

Reprinted in 2001 by:
Nelson Thornes Ltd
Delta Place
27 Bath Road
CHELTENHAM
GL53 7TH
United Kingdom

02 03 04 05 / 10 9 8 7 6 5 4

A catalogue record of this book is available from the British Library

ISBN 0 7487 3599 2

Illustrations by Maureen Carter and Sally Michel
Page make-up by GreenGate Publishing Services

Printed and bound in Great Britain by Ashford Colour Press Ltd, Gosport, Hants.

Acknowledgments

Extracts from *The National Literacy Strategy* produced by the Department for
Education and Employment are Crown copyright reproduced with the permission of
the Controller of Her Majesty's Stationery Office.

**Nelson Thornes publishes a comprehensive range of teacher resource books in the *Blueprints* and *Learning
Targets* series. These titles provide busy teachers with unbeatable curriculum coverage, inspiration and value
for money. For a complete list, please call our Primary Customer Services on 01242 267280, send an e-mail to
cservice@nelsonthornes.com or write to:
Nelson Thornes Ltd, Freepost, Primary Customer Services, Delta Place, 27 Bath Road, Cheltenham GL53 7ZZ.
All Nelson Thornes titles can be bought by phone using a credit or debit card on 01242 267280 or online by
visiting our website – www.nelsonthornes.com**

CONTENTS

Welcome to
LEARNING TARGETS

Learning Targets is a series of practical teacher's resource books written to help you to plan and deliver well-structured, professional lessons in line with all the relevant curriculum documents.

Each Learning Targets book provides exceptionally clear lesson plans that cover the whole of its stated curriculum plus a large bank of carefully structured copymasters. Links to the key curriculum documents are provided throughout to enable you to plan effectively.

The Learning Targets series has been written in response to the challenge confronting teachers not just to come up with teaching ideas which cover the curriculum but to ensure that they deliver high quality lessons every lesson with the emphasis on raising standards of pupil achievement.

The recent thinking from QCA and the National Literacy and Numeracy Strategies on the key factors in effective teaching has been built into the structure of Learning Targets. These might briefly be summarised as follows:

➤➤ that effective teaching is active teaching directed to very clear objectives
➤➤ that good lessons are delivered with pace, rigour and purpose
➤➤ that good teaching requires a range of strategies – including interactive whole class sessions
➤➤ that ongoing formative assessment is essential to planning children's learning
➤➤ that differentiation is necessary but that it must be realistic.

The emphasis in Learning Targets is on absolute clarity. We have written and designed the books to enable you to access and deliver effective lessons as easily as possible, with the following aims:

➤➤ to plan and deliver rigorous, well-structured lessons
➤➤ to set explicit targets for achievement in every lesson that you teach
➤➤ to make the children aware of what they are going to learn
➤➤ to put the emphasis on direct, active teaching every time
➤➤ to make effective use of time and resources
➤➤ to employ the full range of recommended strategies: whole class, group and individual work
➤➤ to differentiate for ability groups realistically
➤➤ to use ongoing formative assessment to plan your next step
➤➤ to have ready access to usable pupil copymasters to support your teaching.

The page opposite provides an at-a-glance guide to the key features of the Learning Targets lessons and explains how they will enable you to deliver effective lessons. The key to symbols on the lesson plans is set out here. ➤➤

How to deliver structured lessons with pace, rigour and purpose

Explicit targets for achievement in every session

The concise subject knowledge you need

Crystal clear lesson plan layouts

The full range of teaching strategies

Rigorous and practical activities

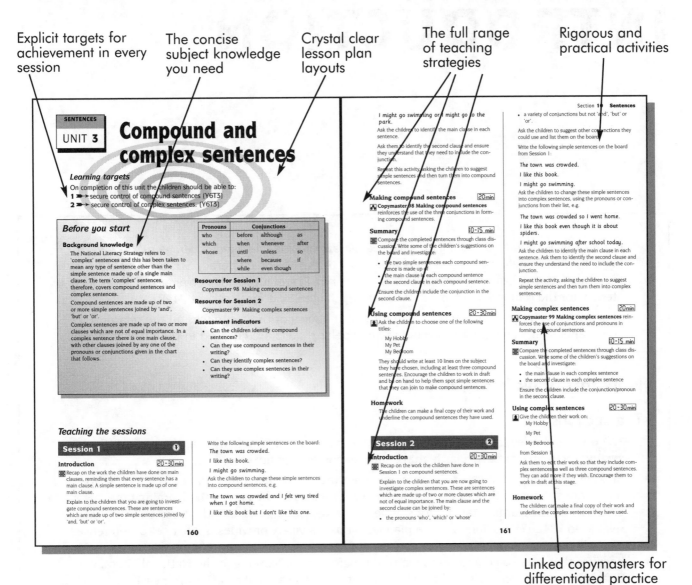

Linked copymasters for differentiated practice and assessment

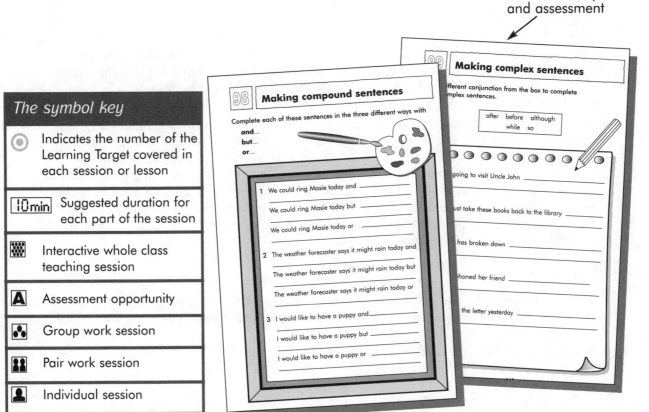

INTRODUCTION

Learning Targets: Grammar and Punctuation Key Stage 2 provides detailed coverage of the part of English which is defined as 'sentence level' work in the National Literacy Strategy. Together with the other Literacy Learning Targets books at this Key Stage, it provides coverage of all aspects of literacy for the National Literacy Strategy at Key Stage 2 and for Scotland P4–P7.

This book covers grammar and punctuation at the level of the sentence. All the related comprehension, composition, decoding and spelling skills are covered in the other books at this level.

How this book is organised

The sections

The book is divided into 10 sections within two main areas, Punctuation and Grammar. Each section focuses on a particular feature, such as commas or adverbs.

In addition we have indicated the principle relevance of each learning target to a term's work in the National Literacy Strategy by a reference in brackets at the end of the learning target. For example, all the learning targets for simple adjectives on page 92 are identified as being mainly related to Y3T2 (Year 3 Term 2). The planner on pages viii–ix provides a fuller set of references. (You will find that some learning targets do not have a year and term reference after them. This is because there are some gaps in the logical progression of learning in the National Literacy Strategy which we felt essential to fill in so that children can make easier progress).

The units

Sections are subdivided into units. Each unit is an integrated piece of work which develops particular grammatical or punctuation skills and knowledge to meet particular learning targets. These learning targets state explicitly what the children should aim to know or be able to do by the end of the unit and provide you with a set of clear, assessable objectives.

Together, the units in a section form an overall set of lesson plans to cover grammar or punctuation. To a certain extent they are 'free-standing' so that you can, for example, use Commas Unit 2 on commas in letters to meet a particular objective within your teaching programme without having undertaken the previous unit on commas in lists. In general, units at the beginning of a section are easier and difficulty builds up incrementally to a mastery of the assessment objectives outlined at the start. Children's progress can be summatively assessed using the assessment copymasters at the end of the section. Advice on using these copymasters is provided in the introduction to each Section.

The sessions

Units are composed of a number of teaching 'sessions'. These teaching suggestions are very specific and detailed, and use the full range of teaching strategies required during the literacy hour: teacher-directed whole class work, individual, pair and group work. Approximate times are suggested to enable you to fit the sessions into your literacy hour programme. In practice, of course, the times actually required will vary according to the children's ability and the way the sessions are going. You will find a key to the symbols used in the sessions on page v.

Within a unit, the sessions tend to increase in complexity. Particular sessions may be used independently of the overall unit for a particular purpose but the sessions within a unit are closely linked, being designed to provide a complete teaching programme which combines grammar and punctuation with best practice in teaching literacy skills. You will probably want to teach the sessions within the context of their whole units.

The copymasters

Photocopiable sheets can be found at the end of every unit and these are integral to teaching the sessions. All the copymasters are reinforced by structured lesson plans.

Using this book alongside the National Literacy Strategy

Learning Targets: Grammar and Punctuation Key Stage 2 has been written to cover the demands of the literacy hour at sentence level and is structured around the learning objectives identifiable in the National Literacy Strategy. The required range of work listed for each term is covered and has been incorporated into the units. While the Strategy document orders work term by term, this entails a high level of repetition and, due to space constraints, *Grammar and Punctuation Key Stage* 2 has ordered material into logical units of literacy work. We have provided a National Literacy Strategy planner (*see* pages viii–x) where material to resource particular needs can be identified term by term.

Each unit of work can supply the material for a string of literacy hours. Units can be broken up into their constituent sessions across the week, using the timings as an approximate guide. Many of the activities and sessions can be used very flexibly across the whole range of learning up to Year 6 and differentiation within the sessions is as much by outcome as by activity. Every teacher will, of course, interpret the demands of the literacy hour individually in the light of their own situation.

Using this book in Scotland

For teachers in Scotland, we have mapped the contents of the units against the relevant attainment targets for reading and writing that relate to grammar and punctuation and these are set out on the Scottish guidelines planner on page x.

Curriculum Planner
National Literacy Strategy planner

This chart shows how you can find activities by section and unit to resource your term by term requirements for sentence level work. On the actual learning targets throughout the book, you will also find term by term references appended. These are the principle NLS locations for particular learning targets. (Because there are some surprising gaps in the logical progression of learning in the NLS for sentence level work you will find that there are some learning targets in the book which appear not to be required in the NLS but which contain essential information for children to master. For example it is essential to understand the concepts of subject, object and predicate in order to be able to understand compound and complex sentences.) The chart below fills in many other references between the NLS and the learning targets.

Year 3 Term 1

Grammatical awareness

2 to take account of the grammar and punctuation when reading aloud: Punctuation – Sentences 1;

3 the function of verbs in sentences through:
- collecting and classifying examples of verbs: Verbs 1;
- experimenting with changing simple verbs in sentences: Verbs 1;
- collecting and classifying examples of verbs: Verbs 1;

5 to use the term 'verb' accurately: Verbs 1;

Sentence construction and punctuation

6 to secure knowledge of question marks and exclamation marks: Punctuation – Sentences 1

7 the basic conventions of speech punctuation: Punctuation – Sentences 2;

8 to use the term 'speech marks': Punctuation – Sentences 2;

Revision and Consolidation from KS1

10 to identify the boundaries between separate sentences: Punctuation – Sentences 1;

12 to demarcate the end of a sentence with a full-stop and the start of a new one with a capital letter: Punctuation – Sentences 1;

13 to use commas to separate items in a list: Commas 1;

Year 3 Term 2

Grammatical awareness

2 the function of adjectives within sentences, through:
- identifying adjectives in shared reading: Adjectives 1;
- collecting and classifying adjectives: Adjectives 1;
- experimenting with deleting and substituting adjectives: Adjectives 1;
- experimenting with the impact of different adjectives through shared writing: Adjectives 1;

3 to use the term 'adjective' appropriately: Adjectives 1;

4 to extend knowledge and understanding of pluralisation through:

- understanding the term 'collective noun': Nouns 2
- noticing which nouns can be pluralised and which cannot: Nouns 1
- recognising pluralisation as one test of a noun: Nouns 1;

5 to use the terms singular and plural appropriately: Nouns 1;

Sentence construction and punctuation

6 to note where commas occur in reading: Commas 1;

7 to use the term 'comma' appropriately: Commas 1;

8 other uses of capitalisation from reading e.g. names, headings: Capitalisation 1, 2;

11 to understand the need for grammatical agreement: Nouns 2; Pronouns 1;

Year 3 Term 3

Grammatical awareness

2 to identify pronouns and understand their functions in sentences: Pronouns 3;
- noticing in speech and reading how they stand in place of nouns: Pronouns 1;
- distinguishing personal pronouns: Pronouns 2;
- substituting pronouns for common and proper nouns: Pronouns 1;
- distinguishing the 1st, 2nd, 3rd person forms of pronouns: Pronouns 1;
- investigating how pronouns are used to mark gender: Pronouns 1;

3 to ensure grammatical agreement in speech and writing of pronouns and verbs: Nouns 2;

Sentence construction and punctuation

4 to use speech marks and other dialogue punctuation appropriately in writing: Punctuation – Sentences 2;

5 how sentences can be joined in more complex ways: Grammar – Sentences 2 and 3;

6 to investigate how words and phrases can signal time sequences: Adverbs 1;

7 to become aware of the use of commas in marking grammatical boundaries: Commas 2;

Year 4 Term 1

Grammatical awareness

2 to revise work on verbs from Year 1 Term 3 and to investigate verb tenses: Verbs 2;

3 to identify the use of powerful verbs: Verbs 1;

4 to identify adverbs and understand their functions in sentences through:
- identifying common adverbs with 'ly' suffix: Adverbs 1;
- noticing where they occur in sentences: Adverbs 1;
- collecting and classifying examples of adverbs: Adverbs 2;
- using adverbs with greater discrimination in own writing: Adverbs 1

Sentence construction and punctuation

5 to practise using commas to mark grammatical boundaries: Commas 2;

Year 4 Term 2

Grammatical awareness

1 to revise and extend work on adjectives:

- constructing adjectival phrases: Adjectives 3;

- examining comparative and superlative adjectives: Adjectives 2;

- comparing adjectives on a scale of intensity: Adjectives 2;

- relating them to suffixes which indicate degrees of intensity: Adjectives 2;

- relating them to adverbs which indicate degrees of intensity: Adjectives 2;

Sentence construction and punctuation

2 to use the apostrophe accurately to mark possession:

- identifying possessive apostrophes: Apostrophes 2;

- understanding basic rules for apostrophising singular and plural nouns: Apostrophes 2;

- to distinguish between the apostrophe for contraction and possession: Apostrophes 1;

- beginning to use the apostrophe appropriately in own writing: Apostrophes 2;

4 to recognise how commas, connectives and full stops are used to join and separate clauses: Grammar – Sentences 2;

Year 4 Term 3

Grammatical awareness

1 to understand that some words can be changed in particular ways: Nouns 1; Verbs 2 and 3;

Sentence construction and punctuation

2 to identify the common punctuation marks: Punctuation – Sentences 1; Apostrophes 1–3; Commas 1–3;

4 the use of connectives, e.g. adjectival phrases, adverbial phrases, conjunctions: Adjectives 3, Adverbs 3, Grammar – Sentences 2 and 3;

Year 5 Term 1

Grammatical awareness

5 to understand the difference between direct and reported speech:

- finding and comparing examples from reading: Punctuation – Sentences 3;

- discussing contexts and reasons for using particular forms: Punctuation – Sentences 3;

- transforming direct into reported speech and vice versa: Punctuation – Sentences 3;

Sentence construction and punctuation

6 to understand the need for punctuation as an aid to the reader: Sentences 1;

7 to understand how dialogue is set out: Sentences 2;

8 to revise and extend work on verbs:

- tenses: Verbs 2;

- forms: Verbs 3;

Year 5 Term 2

Grammatical awareness

4 to revise from Y4:

- the different kinds of nouns: Nouns 3; Nouns 4;

- the function of pronouns: Pronouns 1;

Sentence construction and punctuation

5 to use punctuation effectively to signpost meaning in longer and more complex sentences: Grammar – Sentences 3;

8 to construct sentences in different ways through:

- combining two or more sentences: Grammar – Sentences 2 and 3;

- reordering them: Grammar – Sentences 2 and 3;

9 to secure the use of the comma in embedding clauses within sentences: Adjectives 3;

10 to ensure that, in using pronouns, it is clear to what or to whom they refer: Pronouns 1; Pronouns 3;

Year 5 Term 3

Sentence construction and punctuation

4 to use punctuation marks accurately in complex sentences: Adjectives 3; Grammar – Sentences 2 and 3;

5 to revise use of apostrophes for possession: Apostrophe 2;

6 to investigate clauses through:

- identifying the main clause in a long sentence: Grammar – Sentences 2;

- investigating sentences which contain more than one clause: Grammar – Sentences 2;

- understanding how clauses are connected: Grammar – Sentences 2;

7 to use connectives to link clauses within sentences and to link sentences in longer texts: Grammar – Sentences 2 and 3;

Year 6 Term 1

Grammatical awareness

1 to revise from Y5:

- the different word classes: (all the grammar sections)

- re-expressing sentences in a different order: Grammar – Sentences 2 and 3;

- the construction of complex sentences: Grammar – Sentences 3;

2 to revise earlier work on verbs and to understand the terms active and passive: Verbs 3;

3 to note and discuss how changes from active to passive affect word order and sense: Verbs 3;

Sentence construction and punctuation

4 to investigate connecting words and phrases: Adjectives 3; Grammar – Verbs 3;

5 to form complex sentences: Adjectives 3; Grammar – Sentences 1 and 3;

Year 6 Term 2

Grammatical awareness

1 to investigate further the use of active and passive verbs:

- identify examples of active and passive verbs in texts: Verbs 3;

- experiment in transformation from active to passive: Verbs 3;

- consider how the passive voice can conceal the agent of a sentence: Verbs 3;

Sentence construction and punctuation

3 to revise work on complex sentences:

- identifying main clauses: Grammar – Sentences 2;

- ways of connecting clauses: Grammar – Sentences 3;

- constructing complex sentences: Grammar – Sentences 3;

Year 6 Term 3

Sentence construction and punctuation

3 to revise formal styles of writing:

- the use of the passive – Verbs 3;

- management of complex sentences: Grammar – Sentences 3;

4 to secure control of complex sentences, understanding how clauses can be manipulated to achieve different effects: Grammar – Sentences 2 and 3;

Curriculum Planner
Scottish guidelines planner

As the relevant attainment target statements are quite general in English 5–14, we have simply correlated them against the sections of this book.

WRITING

Punctuation and structure

Pupils should be taught to:

Level B: use capital letters and full stops, and use common linking words; Punctuation – Sentences; Capitalisation;

Level C: punctuate many sentences accurately, including simple use of commas and question marks; begin to use paragraphs; Punctuation – Sentences; Capitalisation; Commas;

Level D: punctuate most sentences accurately; achieve some variety of sentence structure; Punctuation – Sentences; Capitalisation; Apostrophes; Commas;

Level E: construct, punctuate and link sentences of different lengths, and organise in paragraphs; Punctuation – Sentences; Capitalisation; Apostrophes; Commas;

Knowledge about language

Pupils should be taught to:

Level C: show that they know, understand and can use at least the following terms: noun, verb, comma, question mark, purpose, audience; Punctuation – Sentences; Commas; Verbs; Nouns;

Level D: show that they know, understand and can use at least the following terms: adjective, adverb, pronoun and conjunction; masculine and feminine, singular and plural; tense; Pronouns; Adjectives; Adverbs;

Level E: show that they know, understand and can use at least the following terms: subject, predicate, clause; quotation marks, apostrophe; punctuation; Punctuation – Sentences; Apostrophe; Grammar – Sentences;

READING

Pupils should be taught to:

Level C: show that they know, understand and can use at least the following terms: speech marks, exclamation mark; Punctuation – Sentences

SENTENCES

Focus

The first unit in this section recaps on the basic punctuation of sentences, i.e. capital letter, full stop, question mark and exclamation mark, to which the children were introduced in *Grammar and Punctuation Key Stage* 1. Unit 2 extends the work from Key Stage 1 on direct speech, and Unit 3 introduces reported speech.

Content

Unit 1: Basic sentence punctuation

Unit 2: Direct speech

Unit 3: Reported speech

Assessment

At the end of this section children should be able to:

1   demarcate sentences with the appropriate punctuation

2   recognise direct and reported speech

3   punctuate direct speech

4   turn direct speech into reported speech and reported speech into direct speech.

Assessment copymasters

The sentence assessment copymasters are on pages 21–22.

Copymaster 13 Writing a conversation assesses the children's ability to:

- correctly punctuate direct speech in context

- correctly lay out direct speech in context

- use words other than 'said' to signal the speaker.

Copymaster 14 Direct and reported speech assesses the children's ability to turn direct speech into reported speech and reported speech into direct speech.

UNIT 1 | Basic sentence punctuation

Learning targets

On completion of this unit the children should be able to:

1 ➤➤ take account of the grammar and punctuation, e.g. sentences, exclamation marks, when reading aloud (Y3T1)

2 ➤➤ secure knowledge of question marks and exclamation marks in reading, understand their purpose and use appropriately in own writing. (Y3T1)

Before you start

Background knowledge

The basic punctuation of sentences has been introduced in *Learning Targets: Grammar and Punctuation Key Stage 1*, Section 2, Units 1 and 2. Obviously, the teaching and reinforcing of these concepts are ongoing, using the children's own writing as the basis for discussion, but the NLS requires specific revision and consolidation at the beginning of Key Stage 2. The copymasters in these units move away from cloze procedure and adding punctuation. They stimulate children to produce their own writing in which they can demonstrate how well they have grasped these basic concepts. The Key Stage 1 copymasters can be used for children who are having difficulty.

Resources for Session 1

Copymaster 1 Reading sentences
Copymaster 2 Preparing a passage

Resources for Session 2

Copymaster 3 A party invitation
Scenic pictures from magazines showing different parts of the world

Assessment indicators

- Can the children use punctuation to inform their reading?
- Can they devise questions to inform their learning?

Teaching the sessions

Session 1 ❶

Introduction [20min]

▓ Begin by writing several sentences on the board without punctuation. Ensure the sentences, when punctuated, cover full stops, question marks and exclamation marks, e.g.

we built a snowman this morning

the house is on fire

will you play with me

Ask for volunteers to punctuate the sentences, including adding the capital letters.
Spend some time getting the children to read the sentences aloud, using the punctuation as clues, e.g. reading a question in a different way to an exclamation, etc.

Reading punctuation [20min]

⧉ **Copymaster 1 Reading sentences** gives the children the opportunity to practise using punctuation marks to aid reading and to write various forms of sentences for others to read.

Summary [10min]

▓ Ask for volunteers to read the sentences on the copymaster, discussing the different intonation used. The groups can then swap their copymasters to read the sentences they have written.

Preparing a passage [20min]

▣ The children should choose a passage from their current reading book to prepare. Explain that they are going to read the passage to you after they have had time to practise. You will need to be on hand to guide their choice to ensure that there is a range of punctuation in the passage. Alternatively, they can use **Copymaster 2 Preparing a passage**.

Homework

The children can prepare their reading passages at home and can read them to you individually or to the class.

Session 2

Introduction 20-25 min

▨ Session 1, together with the work at Key Stage 1, gives the children opportunities to appreciate the difference between question marks and exclamation marks. This session concentrates on the use of questions to enhance the children's learning.

Discuss why we ask questions, i.e. to gain information. Can the children give you examples of questions they often ask? e.g.

What time is it?

What shall I do next?

Where will I find ...?

Explain to the children that when they are doing topic work, and similar activities, it is useful to think about what they want to know, i.e. to ask themselves questions, so they can write clearly and provide all the information a reader will want to know.

Write this, or another appropriate situation, on the board:

> You have been invited to stay overnight at a friend's house.

Ask the children what information they would need to know, i.e. what questions would they ask? e.g.

What time shall I arrive?

Should I have tea first?

Should I bring a sleeping bag?

Who else will be there?

Are we going out in the evening?

What time should I be picked up next day?

A party invitation 10-15 min

◆ Give each group **Copymaster 3 A party invitation**. The children are required to write a list of questions regarding the party invitation.

Summary 10 min

▨ The children can compare their questions in a class discussion. Emphasise that each question should end with a question mark.

What do I want to know? 15-20 min

▮ The children should repeat the 'party invitation' activity individually with scenic pictures taken from magazines. Each child should look carefully at his or her picture and devise a list of questions he or she would like to ask about the picture. Encourage them to work in draft form initially.

Homework

The children can stick their pictures onto a larger sheet of paper and neatly copy their questions underneath. These can be displayed under the heading 'Asking Questions'.

Reading sentences

How would you read these sentences?

What did you say?

The roof is leaking!

Where did you find that?

Help!

May I sharpen my pencil?

We went shopping on Saturday.

Our cat has had kittens.

I've hurt my foot!

Write a sentence which ends with a full stop.

_____

_____

Write a question.

_____

_____

Write an exclamation.

_____

_____

Read through the passage carefully. Imagine you are going to read this part of the story to a younger child.

Practise how you would read it.

Harry was sometimes a naughty boy. He was five years old and was always in trouble.

One day, Harry was playing with a ball in the garden. He was bored and he decided to look for something more interesting to do. He looked around and saw the dustbin. What do you think he did?

Harry toddled over to the dustbin and began to push it. It rocked backwards and forwards, backwards and forwards. He gave it one more mighty push. The dustbin fell over with a crash! The rubbish tipped out all over the path!

Harry's Mum came rushing out of the house. "What have you done now, Harry?"

She looked at the rubbish. She looked at Harry. "How did the dustbin fall over, Harry?"

"Don't know," said Harry. "I didn't do anything!"

"Harry!"

"I pushed it," Harry mumbled.

"And what are you going to do now?" asked his Mum.

"Pick up the rubbish, I suppose," said Harry.

3 | A party invitation

Kim has received a party invitation but it got wet and the ink has smudged. All she can read is that she has been invited to a party by her friend Sulim. What other information does she need to know?

Come to
my party

From Sulim

R.S.V.P.

Write the questions Kim needs to ask.

_____

_____

_____

_____

_____

_____

_____

_____

UNIT 2 | Direct speech

Learning targets

On completion of this unit the children should be able to:

1 ➤➤ secure the basic conventions of speech punctuation through:
- identifying speech marks in reading
- beginning to use speech marks in own writing
- using capital letters to mark the start of direct speech (Y3T1)

2 ➤➤ use speech marks and other dialogue punctuation appropriately in writing and use the conventions which mark boundaries between spoken words and the rest of the sentence (Y3T3)

3 ➤➤ identify the use of powerful verbs (Y4T1)

4 ➤➤ understand how dialogue is set out, e.g. on separate lines for alternate speakers in narrative and the positioning of commas before speech marks. (Y5T1)

Before you start

Background knowledge

The basic punctuation of direct speech has been introduced in *Learning Targets: Grammar and Punctuation Key Stage* 1, Section 8, Units 1 and 2. Obviously, the teaching and reinforcing of these concepts are ongoing, using the children's own writing as the basis for discussion. However the NLS requires specific revision and consolidation at the beginning of Key Stage 2, to extend the accuracy of speech punctuation throughout the key stage. The Key Stage 1 copymasters can be used for children who are having difficulty.

Resources for Session 1

Copymaster 4 Narrator and character

Copymaster 5 Continuing the story

Resources for Session 2

Copymaster 6 Punctuating direct speech

Copymaster 7 Substitutes for 'said'

Copymaster 8 Practice

Copymaster 9 Extension

Copymaster 10 What did they say?

Assessment indicators

- Can the children identify spoken words, distinguishing them from non-spoken words, i.e. those said by a character speaking and those said by the narrator?

- Can they write a conversation, punctuating direct speech?

- Can they signal the speaker by using a variety of words other than the word 'said'?

Teaching the sessions

Session 1   ① ②

Introduction   20min

▓ Begin by discussing when the children would want to write something that somebody has said, e.g. in stories. Ask how they know that someone is speaking in the stories that they read, i.e. speech marks; signals of 'said', etc.

Ask the class a question, e.g. What time is it?, and write an individual's response on the board, e.g. It's quarter past nine. Ask the class who answered, and write for example 'said Tom'. Ask for a volunteer to add the speech marks and punctuation. Do this activity several times to ensure the children grasp that the speech marks go before and after the spoken words but do not include 'said …'.

Narrator and character   20min

▓▓ Give each pair **Copymaster 4 Narrator and character**, or, alternatively, select suitable passages from current reading books. Ask the children to prepare the passage so they can read it aloud to the class. One child reads the narrator's part, i.e. is the storyteller, and the other reads Mr Jacks' part, i.e. the character in the story. If they are using the copymaster, they can highlight the two parts in different colours.

Summary
[10 min]

The children can read their prepared passages to you, another group of children or the whole class. Recap on how they knew which words Mr Jacks spoke and discuss how speech marks help the reader.

Continuing the story
[25–30 min]

👤 If the children did not use Copymaster 4 in the previous activity, give them each a copy and read it through with them. Explain that they are going to continue the story by writing a conversation which Mr Jacks has with the postman.

The actual layout of dialogue and the use of commas are a later requirement in the NLS and are tackled in the next session, but you can point out to the children that when a different person speaks we begin on a new line. Some of the children will find little problem with this, but what you are essentially looking for at this stage is the correct use of speech marks.

Give each child **Copymaster 5 Continuing the story**, and be on hand to help them as they work and to ensure the conversation is not limited to two lines!

Homework

The children can finish their conversations at home.

Session 2
③ ④

Introduction
[20–25 min]

▦ This session should be tackled when the children have a secure knowledge of speech marks at the beginning and end of spoken words.

Write the following sentences on the board:

"What are you going to do today?" asked Fred.

"Will someone help me!" screamed Paul.

"I must go to the library today," said Kate.

Draw the children's attention to the punctuation at the end of the spoken words. Ask what they notice about it? i.e.

- if the spoken words are a question, they are followed by a question mark
- if the spoken words are an exclamation, they are followed by an exclamation mark
- if the spoken words are an 'ordinary' sentence, they are followed by a comma
- whatever punctuation is used, it goes inside the speech marks.

Write several sentences on the board for individual children to punctuate, e.g.

I need my gloves and scarf today said Emma.

May I borrow your pen asked Mandy.

The river is flooding its banks shouted the farmer.

Emphasise that the punctuation comes inside the speech marks and do not accept answers with the speech marks directly above the question mark or comma. To help them remember, ask the children to decide whether they want a comma, question mark or exclamation mark, write that first and then add the closing speech marks.

Punctuating direct speech
[10–15 min]

👤 Give each child **Copymaster 6 Punctuating direct speech**. This is designed for individual work, but if you feel that some children would benefit from working with a partner ask them to work in pairs.

Summary
[10 min]

Discuss the punctuation the children have used. Where there is not a consensus of opinion, investigate through class discussion why wrong punctuation has been used. This will highlight where children have difficulty recognising various types of sentence (statement, question, exclamation) and/or the difference between narration and spoken words.

Substitutes for 'said'
[15–20 min]

▦/⦿ This is a good opportunity to add extra whole class/group work on words that can be used instead of 'said' in direct speech. This falls into the category of investigating 'powerful' verbs.

Write the following on the board:

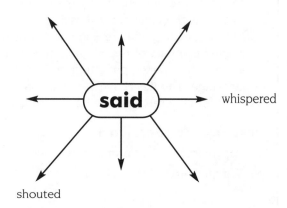

The children can suggest words to complete the web. If this work is tackled in groups, **Copymaster 7 Substitutes for 'said'** can be used. The children can report back in a plenary session. The words can be word processed in different fonts, colours and sizes and displayed on a large sheet of paper as an 'aide memoire' for the children.

Homework

The Practice and Extension Copymasters 8 and 9 can be used for homework. **Copymaster 8 Practice** reinforces the concepts of straightforward speech punctuation. **Copymaster 9 Extension** gives the children two further models on which to base the writing of direct speech, i.e.

- signalling the speaker before the spoken words, e.g.

  Mum asked, "What would you like for breakfast?"

- the spoken words being split by the speaker, e.g.

  "When you have finished," said David, "you can come and help me."

Session 3 ④

⊞ This final session on direct speech concentrates on the layout, i.e. 'separate lines for alternate speakers in narrative'. Some of the children will already have picked this up through the previous sessions and through their own reading, but it is best to spend some time to ensure all the children have grasped it.

Write this piece of text on the board, boxed to look like a piece of paper. Ensure the narrative text goes right across the page.

> Mrs Davies was in the supermarket doing her weekly shopping when she saw Mr Walker.
>
> "Hello," she said.
>
> "Hello," replied Mr Walker.

Ask the children what they notice about the length of the lines of writing. Discuss why a new line starts, i.e. because

- you have reached the edge of the paper
- someone starts speaking
- another person starts speaking.

Can the children devise a rule about new lines in direct speech?

It might be helpful for them to think – *new* person speaking = *new* line. Also, show them that if they ever find themselves writing … " " … then they need to think carefully!

A conversation

👥 Put the children into pairs and give them some starting points for writing a conversation, e.g.

- a shopkeeper and customer
- a teacher and pupil
- a brother and sister.

Explain that they are going to write their conversation on two pieces of paper. Every time they say something they should start a new line. One partner should write in red and the other in blue. When they have finished the conversation, they must check that they have punctuated it correctly. They then cut out each thing they have said and stick it, in order, on another piece of paper so the finished article will have alternate lines of speech in red and blue, e.g.

> "Do you have any tomatoes?" asked Mr Smith.
> **"Yes, fresh in this morning," replied the shopkeeper.**
> "I'll have six please," said Mr Smith.
> **" I'll just weigh them for you," said the shopkeeper.**

Be on hand to check the rough drafts and to encourage the children to edit their work so that not every line of conversation is signalled by 'said'. As an alternative to cutting and sticking, the children can use one piece of paper and write their speech in turn to build up the conversation.

Summary

⊞ The children can read their conversations to the class and they can then be mounted and displayed in the 'Conversation Corner'.

What did they say?

👤 Give each child **Copymaster 10 What did they say?** to work on individually. Encourage the children to work in draft initially on a different piece of paper.

Homework

The children can neatly copy their conversations onto the copymaster, colouring the characters they have chosen. These can then be used for display in the 'Conversation Corner'.

4 | Narrator and character

Read the story carefully to yourself and prepare to read it aloud.
One of you will be the narrator and tell the story.
The other will be Mr Jacks and read everything Mr Jacks says.

At seven o'clock, the alarm went off, just as it always did. Mr Jacks switched it off and climbed out of bed. Just as he was putting on his dressing gown, he heard a loud thud at the front door.

"I wonder what that could be?" said Mr Jacks.

He went downstairs and saw a large envelope lying on the mat.

"Well now, who could be sending me something?" he wondered. Mr Jacks picked up the envelope and read the postmark.

"Cardiff. Who do I know in Cardiff?" he asked himself.

He went through to the kitchen, put the envelope on the table, filled the kettle with water and put it on to boil. He then sat down and stared at the envelope.

"I don't think I know anyone in Cardiff," he muttered. "I suppose the only thing to do is to open it and see what it's all about."

Very carefully, Mr Jacks opened the envelope. Inside was a birthday card and a present wrapped in beautiful gold paper.

"Well I never!" exclaimed Mr Jacks. "I had forgotten it was my birthday!"

He read the card and found out that it was from his brother Tom.

"I must be getting old," he said. "I had forgotten it was my birthday and I had forgotten that my brother Tom has moved to Cardiff!"

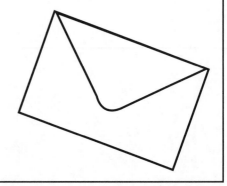

Mr Jacks has just opened his birthday card and present from his brother Tom when he hears a knock at the door. When he opens the door, the postman is there with a large parcel that he forgot to deliver the first time.

Write the conversation that Mr Jacks has with the postman. Remember your speech marks. " "

Punctuating direct speech

Read each sentence carefully.

You will need to add (**speech marks**) and one of the following:

(**a comma**) (**a question mark**) (**an exclamation mark**)

1 Do you know where I put my book asked Claire.

2 Someone has kicked a ball through my window shouted Mrs Hart.

3 We will do silent reading after lunch said Mr Jones.

4 Can you help me enquired Greg.

5 What do you want snapped the old lady.

6 I can't find my homework moaned Sally.

7 I enjoyed going swimming said Tim.

8 Don't be late again warned the teacher.

Substitutes for 'said'

How many words can you think of to use instead of 'said'?

You can look in your reading books.

You can use a thesaurus.

Draw more lines if you need them.

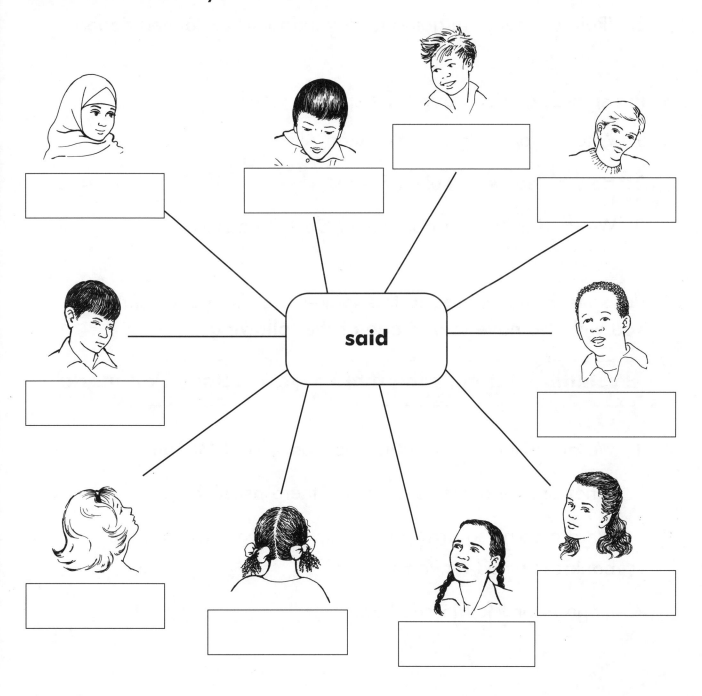

said

Practice

A Underline the spoken words.

1 "I'm sure we will have rain today," said Robert.

2 "The weather forecast said snow," replied Susan.

3 "Rain or snow, I'm going to stay indoors!" exclaimed Robert.

B Put speech marks around the spoken words.

1 What is your dog called? asked Alison.

2 He's called Dex, replied Susan.

3 We used to have a dog called Dex! cried Alison.

C Put speech marks around the spoken words in each sentence. You will also have to add one of the following:

(**a comma**)   (**a question mark**)   (**an exclamation mark**)

1 We are going down to the river today said Mr Toms.

2 What are we going to do down there asked Kim.

3 We are going to draw the plants which grow along the bank explained Mr Toms.

4 Hope I don't fall in cried Sam.

A You know how to write direct speech like this:

"This is an exciting book," said Nathan.

Look what happens to the comma and the full stop if the sentence is turned around:

Nathan said, "This is an exciting book."

Remember – you can use a question mark or an exclamation mark instead of a full stop.

Turn these sentence around.

1 "I'm going for a walk," said Julie.

_____

2 "Where are you going?" asked Chris.

_____

3 "Only to see the horses," replied Julie.

_____

B Sometimes the spoken words are split:

"When I have finished this book," said Dominic, "it will be time for bed."

We need two commas and two lots of speech marks.

Punctuate the following:

1 If it rains tonight said Mark the ground will be too wet to play football.

2 You should leave ten minutes early suggested Dad to make sure you don't miss the bus.

3 I have to go into town said Dad and change my library books.

Choose one of the following and write the conversation you think the characters may have had.

A young boy has kicked his football through an old man's window.

Two friends who have not seen each other for a very long time happen to meet each other in the street.

A brother and sister are planning a surprise birthday party for their mum.

_____

_____

_____

_____

_____

_____

_____

_____

_____

_____

UNIT 3 | Reported speech

Learning target

On completion of this unit the children should be able to:

1 ➤➤ understand the difference between direct and reported speech (e.g. She said, "I am going."/She said she was going.) through:

- finding and comparing examples from reading
- discussing contexts and reasons for using particular forms, and their effects
- transforming direct into reported speech and vice versa, noting changes in punctuation and words that have to be changed or added. (Y5T1)

Before you start

Background knowledge

This unit is a natural extension of Unit 2. It gives children the opportunity to do more work with direct speech and to investigate the reasons for using either direct speech or reported speech.

Turning direct speech into reported speech and vice versa is presented as part of the same session, but it is left to your discretion as to whether this work and the relevant copymasters are split over two sessions.

Resources for Session 1

Reading books with which the children are familiar

Copymaster 11 Direct speech into reported speech

Copymaster 12 Reported speech into direct speech

Assessment indicators

- Can the children recognise direct and reported speech?
- Can they turn direct speech into reported speech?
- Can they turn reported speech into direct speech?

Teaching the session

Session 1 ①

Introduction 20-25 min

▦ Recap on what the children have learned about the punctuation of direct speech.

Write several examples on the board for volunteers to punctuate. Ensure the examples cover the various forms of direct speech. The following are punctuated examples.

"I must learn my spellings today," said Ken.

"Are you going out today?" asked Tom.

"If you put the kettle on," said Mum, "we'll have a cup of tea."

Remind the children that the examples on the board are direct speech because we are hearing/writing/reading the exact words which are spoken.

Another way of expressing speech is through reported speech. Can the children attempt to define what is meant by 'reported speech'? Ensure that at the end of

the discussion the children appreciate that reported speech is when we hear/write/read what someone has said, as told (reported) by someone else.

Use the first example on the board and ask, "What did Ken say?" If the children can only respond by reading the spoken words, prompt them by saying, "Ken said that …".

Compare the two forms, i.e.

"I must learn my spellings today," said Ken.

Ken said that he must learn his spellings today.

in terms of punctuation, word order and word changes.

Do this activity several times as a whole class before beginning group work. If the children grasp the idea quickly, spend some time looking at how reported speech can be turned into direct speech. Alternatively, leave this to be tackled in another whole class session.

During the whole class session discuss with the children the reasons they might use each type of speech, e.g.

- direct speech for characters in stories
- reported speech as one character reports what another character has said.

Working with reading books [20 min]

In groups the children can find examples of direct speech from reading books with which they are familiar. Each child should find an example and, through group discussion, the examples should be turned into reported speech.

You can repeat this activity, asking the children to find examples of reported speech and turn them into direct speech.

Summary [10 min]

Write several examples which the children have found on the board to reinforce the changes needed. Discuss the context of the direct speech examples, e.g.

What has just happened in the story?
Who is speaking?

Who are they speaking to?
What does the direct speech tell the reader?

Discuss the context of the reported speech examples, e.g.

What has just happened in the story?
Who is reporting what another character has said?
Where is that other character at this moment in the story?
What does the reader learn through the reported speech?

Direct and reported speech [20-25 min]

Copymaster 11 Direct speech into reported speech gives the children the opportunity to turn direct speech into reported speech. **Copymaster 12 Reported speech into direct speech** is a similar activity dealing with reported speech being turned into direct speech. The children should tackle both copymasters.

Homework

Work on Copymasters 11 and 12 should be completed for homework.

Change the following examples of direct speech into reported speech.

1 "I don't think there is anyone at home," said the postman.

_____

2 "What do we do if the bus is late?" asked Carol.

_____

3 "The ship is sinking!" shouted the captain.

_____

4 "If we hurry," said May, "we can get into town before the shops close."

_____

_____

5 Roger said, "The film was very good."

_____

6 "You need to copy the sentences on page 43," instructed the teacher.

_____

_____

7 "What is that noise?" complained Claire.

_____

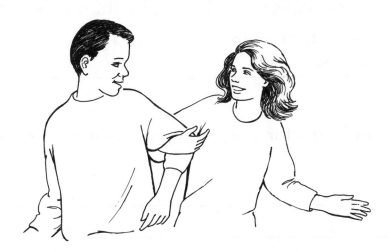

Reported speech into direct speech

Change the following examples of reported speech into direct speech.

1 Mandy wanted to know if the post had arrived.

_____

2 Ian said that he wasn't playing football on Saturday.

_____

3 The teacher said that the children could not go out at playtime.

_____

4 The old man told the driver that the bus was very late.

_____

5 Mum told the twins that they could go for a bicycle ride at the weekend.

_____

_____

6 The policeman remarked that it was the third time that week a window had been broken in the village.

_____

_____

7 The swimming instructor asked all the children to dive to the bottom of the pool.

_____

_____

Rewrite this conversation adding any necessary punctuation.

Use words other than 'said' where you think it will improve the writing and give the reader a clearer picture.

Why does it always seem to rain on a Saturday said Tim. It doesn't always rain on Saturdays said William. Well it's raining today said Tim. What are we going to do? I don't know said William. I suppose we could play a board game or play on the computer. We did that all last Saturday said Tim. Well what do you suggest said William. I think we should go out to play anyway said Tim. You must be joking said William. It's pouring down. We'll get absolutely drenched.

_____

_____

_____

_____

_____

_____

_____

_____

Choose one of the following:

> David's dog has dug holes
> in Mr Black's garden.
> Mr Black has brought the dog
> back to David's house.

> Lyn has to explain to her
> teacher why her homework
> has got holes in it!

Write the conversation between David and Mr Black or between the teacher and Lyn.

_____

_____

_____

_____

_____

_____

Now write what David or Lyn would say if they were reporting the conversation to their parents.

_____

_____

_____

_____

_____

CAPITALISATION

Focus

The first unit in this section revises the use of capitals at the beginning of sentences and for people's names.

Unit 2 looks at other uses of capitalisation, e.g. headings. Take every opportunity to investigate the uses of capitalisation that the children find around them in the classroom whilst you are working through these units, e.g. display headings, book titles.

Content

Unit 1: Revision of capitalisation

Unit 2: Other uses of capitals

Assessment

At the end of this section children should be able to:

1 recognise different uses of capitalisation from reading

2 use capital letters appropriately in their own writing.

Assessment copymasters

The capitalisation assessment copymasters are on pages 31–32.

Copymaster 19 Missing capital letters gives the children the opportunity to rewrite sentences correctly by adding the missing capital letters.

Copymaster 20 Questionnaire gives the children the opportunity to fill in information which requires the use of capital letters.

Revision of capitalisation

Learning target

On completion of this unit the children should be able to:

1 ➡➡ recognise and use capitalisation, e.g. with names. (Y3T2)

Before you start

Background knowledge

Learning Targets: Grammar and Punctuation Key Stage 1 introduced the children to the formation of capital letters within the context of alphabetical order (The alphabet Unit 2); the use of capital letters to begin sentences (Sentences Unit 1) and the concept of proper nouns for the names of people, places, days of the week and months of the year (Nouns Unit 2).

The sessions in this unit revise these earlier concepts and extend the use of capitalisation. During reading sessions, make a point of looking closely at other uses of capitals, e.g. chapter headings/titles, 'shouted' dialogue in capitals, etc.

Resources for Session 1

Copymaster 15 Capital letters

Copymaster 16 Missing capital letters

Assessment indicators

- Can the children recognise capital letters?
- Can they use capital letters appropriately in their own writing for:

  beginning sentences

  people's names

  place names

  days of the week

  months of the year?

Teaching the session

Session 1

Introduction
`20-25 min`

▓ Use this session to revise what the children know about capital letters from Key Stage 1. Ask them when they use capital letters, e.g.
- to begin sentences
- to write people's names
- to write place names
- to write days of the week
- to write months of the year.

Write a variety of words on the board in lower case, e.g.

susan dog table river dee

scotland ben monday

car desk april birmingham

Ask for volunteers to come and correct the words. As each individual child rubs out and adds a capital letter, ask why the word needs a capital letter, e.g.

- because it is someone's name
- because it is a day of the week, etc.

Play the alphabet game. Each child in turn says a proper noun beginning with a letter of the alphabet, e.g.

August
Billy
Cardiff
David
England
Friday …

You can repeat this activity, making it more difficult by stipulating the category, e.g. people's names.

Capital letters
`20 min`

⚫⚫ Give each child **Copymaster 15 Capital letters**. Through group discussion, the children must complete the copymaster using each letter as the first letter of a proper noun.

Summary

 10 min

Through class discussion let the children compare the proper nouns they have chosen. What is the most unusual one for each letter? Has any group used common nouns. If so, discuss why they do not need a capital letter.

Missing capital letters

20-30 min

Copymaster 16 **Missing capital letters** gives the children the opportunity to work individually on correcting a piece of text which has been written without capital letters at the beginning of sentences and for proper nouns. If you wish, the children can simply cross out the inappropriate lower case letters and write the capitals above, or they can copy out the passage with their corrections as a handwriting exercise.

Homework

Copymaster 16 can be completed at home.

Capital letters

Write proper nouns. Use each of these letters as the first letter of a proper noun.

C _____
A _____
P _____
I _____
T _____
A _____
L _____

L _____
E _____
T _____
T _____
E _____
R _____
S _____

This story has all the capital letters missed out.
Write it out neatly, putting in all the capital letters.

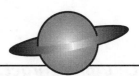

the planet mars was getting closer and closer. harry ford, one of the astronauts, was getting ready for the landing. he was the one who would be first to set foot on the planet. he would leave his space craft virgo and step onto this strange planet.

he and ben green had been in space for many months and all the months had been the same. january, february, march – all the same. there was no weather up in space. all the days seemed the same too, and harry had to check his digital space watch to see that it was monday. he would be standing on the planet mars on a monday morning.

the countdown to the landing began. ten, nine, eight ... and very soon virgo landed with a gentle bump.

Other uses of capitals

Learning target

On completion of this unit the children should be able to:

1 ➤➤ recognise and use capitalisation, e.g. in headings. (Y3T2)

Before you start

Background knowledge

During reading sessions make a point of looking closely at other uses of capitals, e.g. book titles, chapter headings, 'shouted' dialogue in capitals, etc.

Resources for Session 1

Copymaster 17 Headings

Copymaster 18 My own headings

Assessment indicator

- Can the children recognise and use capitalisation for headings?

Teaching the session

Session 1 ①

Introduction 20-25 min

▨ Headings, book titles, etc. may have been suggested by the children in the introductory work to Unit 1 and it is worth spending some time investigating the use of capitals in this context.

There are, seemingly, no hard and fast rules. A heading/title of a display, etc. may read:

> Our Work On The Tudors

or

> Our Work on the Tudors

Look at these two examples with the children. Can they define their own rules for capitalisation in headings? e.g.
'Our' should begin with a capital because it is the first word
'Tudors' should begin with a capital because it is a proper noun
'on' and 'the' are 'little' words so they don't need capitals, etc.

You can also point out that the heading could be written as:

> OUR WORK ON THE TUDORS

Why might all of the heading be in capitals? e.g. visual impact.

Headings 20 min

 In pairs, the children work through **Copymaster 17 Headings**. Encourage them to experiment with the different styles of headings, i.e. the uses of capitals which you have discussed.

Summary 10 min

▨ Ask a child from each group to write one of the headings on the board. Through discussion, compare how each group has written each heading. Allow differences in 'style' but ensure capitalisation for the first word/important words/proper nouns is in place.

My own headings 20-25 min

 Copymaster 18 My own headings gives the children the opportunity to create headings of their own.

Homework

Ask the children to look through newspapers and magazines at home and cut out examples of headings for display. Take some time to look at them and discuss them in terms of capitalisation and general style.

Imagine these are headings on a noticeboard in your classroom.

How would you write them?

- writing about animals

- a visit to blake castle

- our work on shapes

- science experiments

- shape poetry

Make up your own headings for display on a noticeboard in your classroom.

The whole class has been drawing trees.

Several of you have written about your favourite story book.

The class has been working on sound and light.

You have written poetry about outer space.

Missing capital letters

Rewrite each sentence or heading, putting in the missing capital letters.

1   the middle of the week is wednesday.

_____

2   sam, john and peter play football on saturday.

_____

3   we went to spain in august.

_____

4   my birthday is in february.

_____

5   our work on flowers

_____

6   the romans

_____

7   life in tudor times

_____

8   circles, squares and triangles

_____

Questionnaire

Complete this questionnaire. Be careful to use capitals correctly.

Questionnaire

Name

Address _____

_____

_____

Date of birth:

day _____ date _____ month _____ .

Names of brothers and sisters

_____

_____

_____

Names of pets

_____

_____

Places you have visited or would like to visit

_____

_____

_____

APOSTROPHES

Focus

This section introduces the children to the two uses of the apostrophe, i.e. contraction and possession, giving them the opportunity to identify apostrophes from reading, investigate the uses of the apostrophe and use apostrophes appropriately in their own writing.

Content

Unit 1: Apostrophe of contraction

Unit 2: Apostrophe of possession

Assessment

At the end of this section children should be able to:

1 identify when an apostrophe is signalling (an) omitted letter(s)

2 identify when an apostrophe is signalling possession

3 use both the apostrophe of contraction and the apostrophe of possession in their own writing.

Assessment copymasters

The apostrophe assessment copymasters are on pages 45–46.

Copymaster 28 Apostrophe of contraction gives the children the opportunity to:

• correctly punctuate sentences using the apostrophe of contraction

• use shortened forms in their own writing.

Copymaster 29 Apostrophe of possession gives the children the opportunity to identify singular and plural owners and to use the apostrophe of possession in sentences of their own.

UNIT 1 | Apostrophe of contraction

Learning targets

On completion of this unit the children should be able to:

1 ➤➤ recognise the apostrophe of contraction in reading
2 ➤➤ use the apostrophe of contraction appropriately in their own writing. (Y4T2)

Before you start

Background knowledge

Of the two, the apostrophe of contraction causes fewer problems as long as the children securely grasp that the apostrophe takes the place of a missing letter or letters. They should also be made aware that contracted forms are more appropriate in speech than in writing.

Resources for Session 1

Copymaster 21 Using apostrophes

Copymaster 22 A conversation

Assessment indicators

- Can the children identify the apostrophe of contraction in their reading?
- Can they use the apostrophe to write shortened forms?

Teaching the session

Session 1 ① ②

Introduction 　20–25 min

▨ Begin by investigating whether the children are aware of apostrophes in their reading. Can they find examples and explain why they are there?

Write several examples on the board. It is a good idea to use direct speech for these examples and to discuss with the children why they are more appropriate in speech than in writing, e.g.

"Don't forget about Tuesday," said Nick.

"I can't unlock the door," complained Liz.

"I'm sure I left my book here," moaned Oliver.

Take each example in turn and ask the children to find the word that they could write in a different way/has been shortened. Hopefully, they will pick out:

don't　　do not
can't　　cannot
I'm　　　I am

Use coloured chalk to show the relationship between the omitted letter(s) and the apostrophe.

Ask the children for other word examples. If they give a shortened form, ask another child to 'expand' it and vice versa.

Ask the children to suggest other sentences with shortened forms. Write them on the board and examine the apostrophised word in the same way. If all the examples are 'not'/'__n't' suggest a few of your own to include examples such as 'you are'/'you're', 'he is'/'he's', 'they are'/'they're', etc. Ensure that they also examine 'will not'/'won't', 'shall not'/'shan't'.

Using apostrophes 　15 min

▨ Give each child a copy of **Copymaster 21 Using apostrophes**, but allow them to complete them through group discussion if they wish. Ask the children to ring/highlight/ underline the letters they will miss out and then write the shortened form on the line in each 'cloud'.

Summary 　10 min

▨ Volunteers from each group can write their answers on the board. The children can compare their answers through class discussion.

One recurring problem that many children have is putting the apostrophe in the right place, i.e. in place of the missing letter(s). You may find some children writing 'would'nt', 'must'nt', etc.

Spend some time reinforcing the idea that the children should first look for letters that are missed out so they learn to place the apostrophe correctly, e.g.

would **not**　wouldn't
must **not**　mustn't

A conversation

`20-25 min`

Give each child **Copymaster 22 A conversation**. The children are required to write a conversation in the speech bubbles, using as many of the contracted words in the box as possible. Be on hand to help them 'get started' by discussing with individuals what their conversation could be about.

Homework

The children can complete Copymaster 22 at home. If they have finished it in class, they can write out the conversation as direct speech with the correct punctuation.

Using apostrophes

Write the short form of these words.

Remember your apostrophes!

he is

_____

you are

_____

I have

_____

shall not

_____

would not

_____

she had

_____

must not

_____

they are

_____

it is

_____

he will

_____

A conversation

Write conversations in the speech bubbles using as many of the words from the box as you can.

I'm   we'll   can't   you're
don't   won't   it's
they're   he's

UNIT 2 | Apostrophe of possession

Learning target

On completion of this unit the children should be able to:

1 ➡➡➡ use the apostrophe accurately to mark possession through:
- identifying possessive apostrophes in reading and to whom or what they refer (Y4T2)
- understanding basic rules for apostrophising singular nouns, e.g. 'the man's hat', for plural nouns ending in 's', e.g. 'the doctors' surgery' and for irregular plural nouns, e.g. 'men's room', 'children's playground' (Y4T2)
- distinguishing between uses of the apostrophe for contraction and possession (Y4T2)
- beginning to use the apostrophe appropriately in their own writing. (Y4T2)

Before you start

Background knowledge

The apostrophe of possession can cause problems, so be prepared to find some children using it whenever there is an 's' on the end of a word, as they confuse a straightforward plural with an 'owner'. Spend as much time as possible working orally so that the children can see themselves as owners and understand what the apostrophe, in this context, is signalling.

Session 1 deals with the apostrophe of possession when the owner is singular, e.g. 'the girl's coat'. Session 2 deals with plural owners ending in 's', e.g. 'the girls' coats', and with irregular plurals, e.g. 'the men's boots'.

Resources for Session 1

Copymaster 23 Find the owner

Copymaster 24 Using apostrophes

Copymaster 25 Shorter sentences

Resources for Session 2

Copymaster 26 Find the owner

Copymaster 27 Using apostrophes

Assessment indicators

- Can the children identify the apostrophe of possession?
- Can they correctly use the apostrophe of possession to signal singular and plural owners?

Teaching the sessions

Session 1 ➊

Introduction   20–25 min

▨ Recap on the use of the apostrophe to signal missing letters and explain to the children that you are going to look at another way of using apostrophes. Write the following example on the board:

John's dog is called Sandy.

Draw the children's attention to 'John's' and explain that John owns/has something. Ask: What does John own?

We could write the sentence like this:

The dog belonging to John is called Sandy.

'John's dog' means the same as 'the dog belonging to John'.

We add 's to the owner to show he/she/it owns/has something. This apostrophe is called the apostrophe of possession as it shows someone owns/possesses something.

Write the following examples on the board:

The cat belonging to Mandy has gone missing.

The leaves belonging to the tree have fallen off.

The wings belonging to the insect are blue.

Ask for volunteers to underline the owner in each sentence, i.e.

Mandy

tree

insect

Remind the children that the sentences can be written in a different way by adding **'s** to the owner, i.e.

Mandy's cat has gone missing.

The tree's leaves have fallen off.

The insect's wings are blue.

Spend some time using the children as 'living' examples, e.g.

This is the pencil belonging to Sam.

Whose pencil is it?

Write the children's response on the board, i.e.

Sam's pencil

Find the owner   `15-20 min`

Give each pair **Copymaster 23 Find the owner**. The children should underline the owner in each case. The first half of the copymaster gives picture clues. Remind the children that if they 'expand' each one, i.e. '_____ belonging to _____', it will help them find the owner.

Summary   `10 min`

Compare the children's answers through class discussion and investigate any problems.

Using apostrophes   `20-25 min`

Give each child **Copymaster 24 Using apostrophes** to punctuate. Remind the children that they should decide who the owner is in each sentence and not just put apostrophes before every 's'!

Homework

The children can finish the copymaster at home. For those who have finished in class, **Copymaster 25 Shorter sentences**, will provide further practice in using the apostrophe of possession.

Session 2   ❶

Introduction   `20-25 min`

Recap on what the children have learned in Session 1, working through a few oral examples. Explain to the children that the work they have been doing has been about a singular owner, i.e. one boy, one dog, one tree, etc. You are now going to look at how to use the apostrophe when the owner is plural/more than one.

Write the following example on the board:

The bird's nest was in the hedge.

Explain that the owner is 'the bird' and the **'s** has been added to show it owns the nest.

Now write:

The birds' nest was in the hedge.

What do the children notice about where the apostrophe is?

Explain that because the 's' is before the apostrophe, the owner is the word 'birds'. More than one bird owns this nest.

Work through some more examples on the board, asking the children to identify the owners, e.g.

The cats' tails were dirty.   (Owner = cats)

The boys' boots were muddy.   (Owner = boys)

The farmers' fields were flooded.   (Owner = farmers)

At this point you can introduce words which do not form their plurals with an 's', e.g.

men   women   children   feet   teeth.

Explain that if the plural word has no 's' then we add **'s** to show ownership, e.g.

the men's cars

the women's houses

the children's toys

Find the owner   `15-20 min`

Give each pair **Copymaster 26 Find the owner**. The children should underline the owner in each case. The first half of the copymaster gives picture clues. Remind the children that all the owners are plural.

Summary   `10 min`

Compare the children's answers through class discussion and investigate any problems.

Using apostrophes   `20-25 min`

Give each child **Copymaster 27 Using apostrophes** to punctuate. Remind the children that they should decide if the owner is singular or plural before adding apostrophes.

Homework

The children can complete the copymaster at home.

Find the owner

Underline the owner.

the girl's coat

the dog's bone

the bird's wing

Mum's bicycle

Dad's chair

the baby's rattle

Tim's books   the ship's crew   the fox's den

the man's luggage   the caterpillar's legs

the sun's rays   the snowman's head

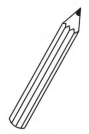

my brother's room   her sister's gloves

Find the owner in each sentence.

Add the apostrophe.

1 The boxes are in Peters shed.

2 Where have you put the dogs bowl?

3 Alis room is a mess.

4 I have found a birds nest.

5 The castles walls are in ruins.

6 Did you find Mums glasses?

7 Richards pen was leaking.

8 A womans bag was left on the bus.

Rewrite these sentences using the apostrophe to show the owner.

1 John knocked over the bowl belonging to the cat.

_____

2 The wing belonging to the bird was broken.

_____

3 The book belonging to Kate was on the shelf.

_____

4 The football belonging to Paul had burst.

_____

5 The garden belonging to Mr Smith was overgrown.

_____

6 The letter belonging to Harry arrived that day.

_____

7 The kitten belonging to Mary was called Spike.

_____

8 The drawbridge belonging to the castle was dangerous.

_____

Find the owner

Underline the owner.

the girls' scarves   the dogs' bones   the birds' beaks

the cats' claws   the men's sticks   the babies' hats

the children's swing   the goats' field

the women's cases   the rabbits' hutch

the flowers' leaves   the foxes' den   my brothers' room

our parents' car   the elephants' trunks

the nurses' uniform

Find the owner or owners in each sentence.

Put the apostrophe in the correct place.

1 The boys coats were on the floor.

2 The childrens stories were put on the wall.

3 The tigers foot was hurt.

4 The captains ship was ready to sail.

5 The books cover was torn.

6 The animals cages had to been cleaned out.

7 The clocks chime was very loud.

8 The girls mother came to pick them up.

9 The trees trunks were enormous.

10 The policemens car was parked by the supermarket.

Apostrophe of contraction

A Put in the missing apostrophes.

1 "I dont want sandwiches," said Lucy.

2 "You mustnt play near the road," warned the teacher.

3 "Its going to snow today," said the weather man.

4 "Were not going until tomorrow," announced Mum.

5 "Well post the letter this afternoon," said Dad.

B Use these words in sentences of your own.

can't   she'll   we've   haven't

A Rewrite these sentences using **'s** or **s'** to show the owner or owners.

1   The bicycles belonging to the girls had been cleaned.

   _____

2   The pen belonging to the boy was leaking.

   _____

3   The umbrellas belonging to the men dripped on the floor.

   _____

4   The bedding belonging to the hamster needed changing.

   _____

B Use these words in sentences of your own.

(ladies')   (snake's)   (people's)   (shop's)

_____

_____

_____

_____

_____

_____

_____

_____

COMMAS

Focus

The units in this section introduce two specific uses of the comma:

1 lists

2 greetings and endings in letters.

Commas used to separate spoken words from the rest of the sentence can be found in Section 1 Unit 2: Direct speech.

Commas used to mark grammatical boundaries in sentences, i.e. clauses, can be found in Sections 7 and 9 where adverbial and adjectival clauses are investigated.

Content

Unit 1: Commas in lists

Unit 2: Commas in letters

Assessment

At the end of this section children should be able to:

1 recognise commas in reading, pausing appropriately

2 use commas when writing lists and letters.

Assessment copymaster

The assessment copymaster is on page 55 and can be used to assess all the punctuation in the first four sections of the book.

Assessment Copymaster 34 Punctuation gives the children an opportunity to punctuate a piece of dialogue and a letter.

Commas in lists

Learning target

On completion of this unit the children should be able to:

1 ➡ use commas to separate items in a list. (Y3T1)

Before you start

Background knowledge

Children will probably have come across the use of commas in lists. Therefore this session combines this with revision of the use of 'and' and 'but' to join the last two items. Wherever possible, encourage the children to use expressive, imaginative vocabulary to ensure that this concept is grasped in an interesting, lively context. Throughout, stress that commas are used when the list is within a sentence as opposed to a vertical column of words as in a shopping list, for example.

Resources for Session 1

Copymaster 30 Writing lists

Copymaster 31 Lists in sentences

Assessment indicators

- Can the children recognise that the comma signals a short pause in reading?
- Can they use commas when they write lists?

Teaching the session

Session 1 ①

Introduction [15min]

▓ Begin by writing a large comma on the board. Ask the children:

Do you know what this is?
Do you know what it signals when you are reading?
Can you give examples of when it is used?

Explain that the comma is a punctuation mark which is used to show the reader when to pause. It signals a shorter pause than a full stop.

Write the following on the board to show how the comma is used in lists:

The cave was damp, dark, frightening and cold.

Ask the children to pick out the words which describe the cave. Ask: does a comma separate all the words that describe the cave?

Give the children another example to investigate and see if they can 'discover' the rule, i.e. items in a list are separated by commas except for the last two where a conjunction is usually used.

Write an example on the board which uses 'but', e.g.

I like peas, carrots and beans but not sprouts.

Revise the use of 'and' and 'but' – 'and' is used when something is expected and 'but' when something is unexpected (see *Learning Targets: Grammar and Punctuation Key Stage 1*, Section 7, Unit 1).

Writing lists [15–20min]

●●● Put the children into groups of four. Give each group **Copymaster 30 Writing lists**. Each child in the group should contribute a word to the list and, through group discussion, they should decide on where the commas go.

Summary [10min]

▓ Let the children compare their lists through class discussion. Comment on any interesting or unusual vocabulary. Has each group provided an appropriate item to follow 'and' and 'but'?

The groups can swap copymasters and read each other's. Encourage them to pause slightly at each comma.

Sentence lists [20min]

▉ Give each child **Copymaster 31 Lists in sentences**. The children are required to use the words to make lists in sentences. Explain that they can categorise the words in different ways, e.g.

- likes
- dislikes
- alphabetical order
- words beginning with the same letter, etc.

The children should have at least three words in each list and they should try to use all the words at least once. Remind them to check carefully that they have used the commas correctly.

Homework

The children can finish the copymaster at home. For those who have finished in class, ask them to write some sentences where all the words used in the list begin with the same letter. Give the following example as a model:

The dog was brown, bold, big and beautiful.

| **Writing lists**

Finish each sentence by making a list and using commas.

1 The monster is _____ _____ _____ and _____

2 The bicycle is _____ _____ _____ and _____ .

3 This food is _____ _____ _____ but _____ .

4 My dog is _____ _____ _____ but _____ .

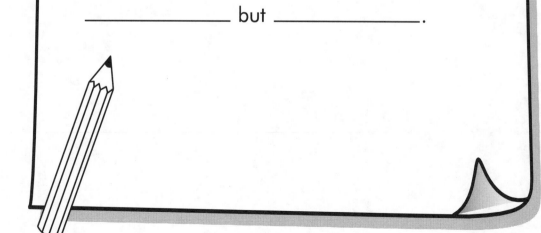

31 | Lists in sentences

Use these words to write some sentences with lists.

Use at least three words in each sentence list.

chocolate	fox	camel
dirty	old	empty
rain	cream	elephant
bread	snow	wind

_____

_____

_____

_____

_____

_____

_____

_____

_____

_____

Commas in letters

Learning target

On completion of this unit the children should be able to:

1 ➡ use commas in the context of letter writing. (Y3T3)

Before you start

Background knowledge

This is a very simple concept which most children will grasp. Letter writing is introduced in *Learning Targets: Non-fiction Key Stage 2 Years 3 and 4*, Unit 7 and this unit will serve to reinforce the use of the comma and the correct greetings and endings for different types of letters.

Resources for Session 1

Copymaster 32 Greetings and endings
Copymaster 33 Letter writing frame

Assessment indicators

- Can the children recognise that the comma signals a short pause in reading?
- Can they use commas appropriately for the greeting and ending of a letter?

Teaching the session

Session 1   ①

Introduction   `15-20 min`

▓ Recap on what the children already know about commas, i.e. that they signal a short pause in reading and are used to separate items in a list.

Write the following on the board:

> Dear Nan
> Thank you for the socks jumper and book which you sent me for my birthday.
> Lots of love
> Harry

Ask the children to help you punctuate the letter. Hopefully, they will recognise the short list within the letter and some children will know to add a comma after 'Nan' and 'love' from their own experience of letters. Spend some time discussing the greetings and endings of letters, i.e.

1 When the writer knows the name of the person they are writing to but does not know them personally:

> Dear Mr Green,
> Yours sincerely,

2 When the writer knows the person they are writing to very well:

> Dear Susan,
> Lots of love,
> Best wishes,
> See you soon,

3 When the writer does not know the name of the person they are writing to:

> Dear Sir or Madam,
> Yours faithfully,

Greetings and endings   `10-15 min`

◆◆ Give each group **Copymaster 32 Greetings and endings**. Through group discussion, the children should decide on how they would begin and end each letter.

Summary   `10 min`

▓ Individuals from each group can write their greetings and endings on the board. Discuss the appropriateness of their choice and the use of the comma.

Writing a letter   `20-30 min`

👤 Give each child **Copymaster 33 Letter writing frame** and choose a context for the letter which is relevant to current topic work. The frame should be used for planning and drafting the letter.

Homework

The children can write a neat copy of their letter for homework.

How would you begin and end these letters?

A letter to your favourite uncle

A letter of complaint to the manager of a local supermarket

INK

A letter to your best friend

A letter to the editor of your favourite magazine

33 Letter writing frame

(address)

____

____

____

____

(greeting)

____

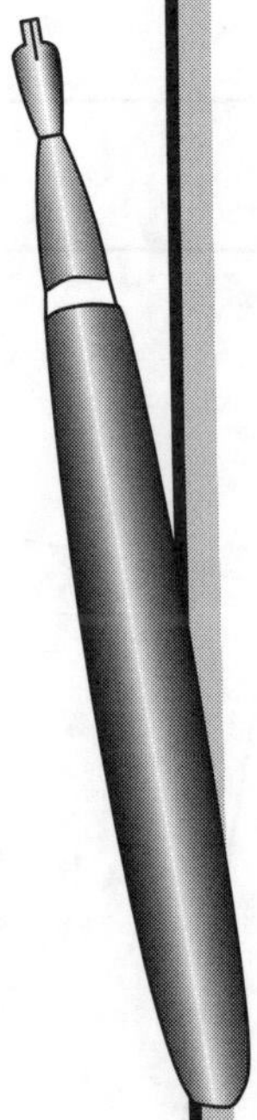

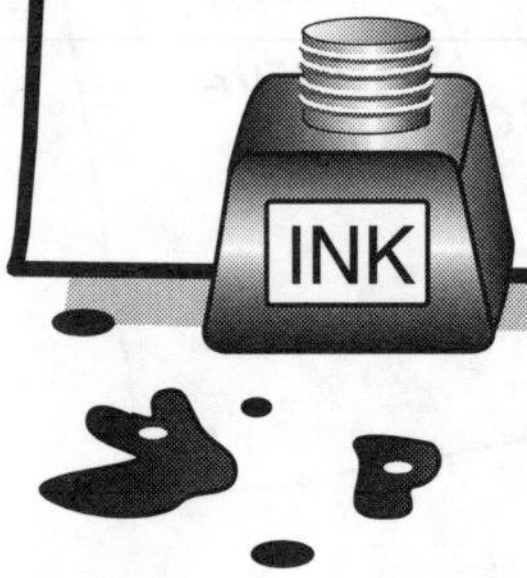

(ending) ____________________

Add the missing punctuation.

It was a very cold day in December William Harry and Lisa were walking home from school

It might snow tonight said Lisa

Hope so replied William Its Saturday tomorrow so we could get the sledges out

It wont snow that much Harry said It will probably just ...

You never know interrupted Lisa Remember the snow last year

Yes It only snowed for one day and it was really deep said William

I remember cried Harry We built a snowman a fort and a wall and had a snowball fight

Add the missing punctuation.

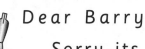

Dear Barry

Sorry its been so long since I have written Things here are much the same We went back to school on Tuesday I always hate going back after the Christmas holidays Ill write more when I have some interesting news to tell you

Best wishes

James

NOUNS

Focus

The children have met the term 'noun' in *Learning Targets: Grammar and Punctuation Key Stage* 1, Section 3, where common and proper nouns were introduced.

The units in this section cover common ways of forming plural nouns, collective nouns, abstract nouns and compound nouns. Opportunities should be given throughout the sessions for using these types of nouns in the context of writing and for emphasising noun/verb agreement.

Contents

Unit 1: Pluralisation

Unit 2: Collective nouns

Unit 3: Abstract nouns

Unit 4: Compound nouns

Assessment

At the end of this section children should be able to:

1 use the terms 'singular' and 'plural' appropriately

2 recognise pluralisation as one test of a noun

3 be able to identify and use collective, abstract and compound nouns.

Assessment copymasters

The sentence assessment copymasters are on pages 73–74.

Copymaster 44 Making plurals requires the children to write the plural endings for nouns correctly.

Copymaster 45 Categorising nouns requires the children to sort a set of nouns into their correct noun categories. Obviously some of the common nouns are also compound and/or abstract nouns, so give the children the instruction to look for the compound and/or abstract nouns first.

UNIT 1 | Pluralisation

Learning targets

On completion of this unit the children should be able to:

1 ➡ recognise pluralisation as one test of a noun (Y3T2)

2 ➡ notice which nouns can be pluralised and which cannot (Y3T2)

3 ➡ use the terms 'singular' and 'plural' appropriately. (Y3T2)

Before you start

Background knowledge

This unit covers basic forms of pluralisation, i.e.

Session 1:   adding 's' and 'es'

Session 2:   nouns ending in 'y' and nouns with irregular plural endings

Session 3:   nouns ending in 'f'/'fe'

This work on plural nouns is linked to verb/noun agreement.

Resources for Session 1

Copymaster 35 Plurals 1

large sheets of paper

newspapers and magazines

Resources for Session 2

Copymaster 36 Plurals 2

large sheets of paper

newspapers and magazines

Resources for Session 3

Copymaster 37 Plurals 3

large sheets of paper

newspapers and magazines

Assessment indicators

• Can the children use the term 'singular' and 'plural' appropriately?

• Can they form plural nouns correctly?

Teaching the sessions

Session 1 ①

Introduction   20-25 min

▦ Begin by recapping on what the children understand by the term 'noun'. Ask for examples of common and proper nouns.

Select some of the children's suggestions which form their plurals by adding 's' and write them on the board, e.g.

one desk   one book   one pen   one chair

two _____   three_____   four_____   five_____

Ask for volunteers to fill in the gaps.

Explain that one 'desk', one 'book', etc. are singular nouns – i.e. just one.

Two 'desks', three 'books', etc. are plural nouns – i.e. more than one.

Now write the following on the board:

one bus   one match one bush one fox

two_____   three_____   four_____   five_____

Can any of the children fill in the gaps? All these words form their plurals with 'es' because they end in 's','ch','sh', or 'x'.

Ask the children to help you compile a list of other words which form their plural in 'es', e.g.

s	ch	sh	x
class	witch	wish	box
glass	torch	dish	tax
cross	finch	rash	
mass	punch	gash	
gas	church	marsh	

To complete the 's'/'es' form of plurals look at words ending in 'o' and 'oo'.

For most words ending in 'o' the plural is formed by adding 'es', e.g.

tomato   tomatoes

potato   potatoes

For nouns that are the names of musical instruments and end in 'o', the plural is formed by adding 's'. Ask the children to help you compile a list of musical words ending in 'o', e.g.

piano	pianos
cello	cellos
piccolo	piccolos

Words ending in 'o' that are shortened forms also form their plural by adding 's', e.g.

| hippo | hippos |
| photo | photos |

Nouns ending in 'oo' also form their plural by adding 's', e.g.

| bamboo | bamboos |
| cockatoo | cockatoos |

Plural posters   `20min`

The children can work in groups to make 'plural' posters. They should head large sheets of paper with the following:

S   ES   O

They can write plural words on the appropriate poster, or cut out plural words from newspapers and magazines. This can be an ongoing activity which can be displayed in the classroom as a reference.

Summary   `10-15 min`

Use this time to look at the posters and to introduce the idea of noun/verb agreement. Using the words on the posters investigate the correct use of 'is'/'are', 'was'/'were'. Choose several nouns and write their singular and plural forms on the board, e.g.

The book	The books
The witch	The witches
The fox	The foxes

Explain that these are the beginnings of sentences which should be completed by using either 'is'/'are' or 'was'/'were'. Ask the children to make suggestions to complete the sentences, e.g.

The book is on the shelf.
The books are on the floor.
The witch was chased away.
The witches were kind.

Plurals   `15-20min`

Give each child **Copymaster 35 Plurals 1**. The work is in two sections. Section one requires the children to form plurals and section two to complete sentences.

Homework

The children can

- complete the copymaster for homework
- look for examples of plural nouns ('s'/'es') in news-papers and magazines to add to their posters.

Session 2   ① ② ③

Introduction   `15-20min`

Remind the children of the 's'/'es' work from the last session. Explain that they are going to look at two more ways in which nouns can form their plurals, i.e. nouns ending in 'y' and nouns which have irregular plurals.

Ask the children to suggest nouns which end in 'y' and write them on the board, e.g.

baby	puppy
toy	city
boy	

Write the following headings:

IES   S

Can the children form the plural of these nouns and classify them under the appropriate headings?

babies	toys
puppies	boys
cities	

Use these examples to investigate the rule about the pluralisation of nouns ending in 'y'. The rule is: If the letter before the 'y' is a vowel add 's'; If the letter before the 'y' is a consonant, drop the 'y' and add 'ies'.

Can the children now add more plurals under each heading? e.g.

cherries	keys
diaries	days
lilies	trays
ladies	bays
armies	rays
ponies	ways

Move on to looking at nouns which have a different word as their plural. Write the singular form of such words on the board, e.g.

one child	two _____
one person	three _____
one foot	four _____

Can the children fill in the gaps?

Can they add more examples to the list? e.g.

woman	ox
man	mouse
tooth	postman
geese	

Plural posters   `20min`

In groups, the children can make two more plural posters. They should head large sheets of paper with the following:

Y – S   Y – IES

The children can write plural words on the appropriate poster, or cut out plural words from newspapers and magazines. This can be an ongoing activity which can be displayed in the classroom as a reference.

Summary
`10-15 min`

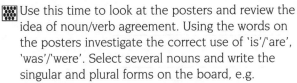 Use this time to look at the posters and review the idea of noun/verb agreement. Using the words on the posters investigate the correct use of 'is'/'are', 'was'/'were'. Select several nouns and write the singular and plural forms on the board, e.g.

The baby	The babies
The day	The days
The pony	The ponies

Explain that these are the beginnings of sentences which should be completed by using either 'is'/'are' or 'was'/'were'. Ask the children for suggestions and complete the sentences, e.g.

The baby is crying.

The babies are crying.

The day was cold and wet.

The days were cold and wet.

Plurals
`15-20 min`

Give each child **Copymaster 36 Plurals 2**. The work is in two sections. Section one requires the children to form plurals and section two to complete sentences.

Homework

The children can

- complete the copymaster for homework
- look for examples of plural nouns ('s'/'ies') in newspapers and magazines to add to their posters.

Session 3   ① ② ③

Introduction
`15-20 min`

The last group of nouns in this unit are those which end in 'f' or 'fe'.

Follow the same format as Sessions 1 and 2, to investigate the following nouns:

calf	calves
elf	elves
half	halves
knife	knives
life	lives
loaf	loaves
scarf	scarves
sheaf	sheaves
shelf	shelves
thief	thieves
wolf	wolves

For some 'f' and 'fe' nouns the plural is formed by adding 's' and it is a good idea to ask the children to learn these and ensure they are familiar with the meaning:

chief	chiefs
cliff	cliffs
dwarf	dwarfs
gulf	gulfs
handkerchief	handkerchiefs
muff	muffs
oaf	oafs
reef	reefs
roof	roofs
sheriff	sheriffs
waif	waifs

Plural posters
`20 min`

 In groups, the children can make two more plural posters. They should head large sheets of paper with the following:

F/FE – S   F/FE – VES

The children can write plurals on the appropriate poster, or cut out plural words from newspapers and magazines. This can be an ongoing activity which can be displayed in the classroom as a reference.

Summary
`10-15 min`

Use this time to look at the posters and review the idea of noun/verb agreement. Using the words on the posters investigate the correct use of 'is'/'are', 'was'/'were'. Select several nouns and write the singular and plural form on the board, e.g.

The loaf	The loaves
The thief	The thieves
The roof	The roofs

Explain that these are the beginnings of sentences which should be completed by using either 'is'/'are' or 'was'/'were'. Ask for suggestions and complete the sentences, e.g.

The loaf is mouldy.

The loaves are mouldy.

The thief was caught red-handed.

The thieves were caught red-handed.

Plurals
`15-20 min`

Give each child **Copymaster 37 Plurals 3**. The work is in two sections. Section one requires the children to form plurals and section two to complete sentences.

Homework

The children can

- complete the copymaster for homework
- look for examples of plural nouns ('s'/'ves') in newspapers and magazines to add to their posters
- learn the plural spelling of the 'f'/'fe' words which form their plurals with 's'.

59

A Write the plural nouns.

bird _____   watch _____

flash _____   fox _____

crab _____   glass _____

piano _____   hippo _____

tree _____   ditch _____

B Complete these sentences using **is**, **are** or **was**, **were** as appropriate.

1 Today it _____ Susan's birthday.

2 Two of the dresses _____ torn.

3 Most of the beaches on this part of the coast _____ clean.

4 Three coaches _____ waiting outside the school.

5 The football pitch _____ too muddy to play on.

A Write the plural nouns.

key _____

ox _____

lorry _____

diary _____

tooth _____

chimney _____

hobby _____

motorway _____

woman _____

valley _____

B Complete these sentences with **is**, **are** or **was**, **were**.

1 The people _____ queuing at the bus stop.

2 Three geese _____ waddling across the road.

3 The keys _____ on the table.

4 Some of the cherries _____ ripe.

5 Four puppies _____ born in the night.

is   are   was   were

Plurals 3

A Write the plural nouns.

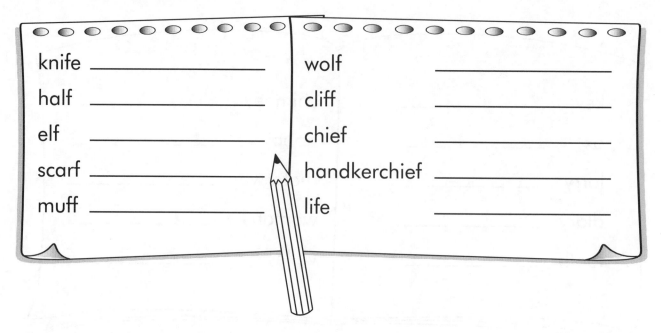

knife _____

half _____

elf _____

scarf _____

muff _____

wolf _____

cliff _____

chief _____

handkerchief _____

life _____

B Complete these sentences with **is**, **are** or **was**, **were**.

1 The leaves _____ falling from that tree.

2 There _____ seven dwarfs in this story.

3 The shelves _____ full of books.

4 There _____ wolves in Britain many years ago.

5 Many roofs in the town _____ covered with snow.

UNIT 2 | Collective nouns

Learning targets

On completion of this unit the children should be able to:

1 ➡️ understand the term 'collective noun' and collect examples – experiment with inventing other collective nouns (Y3T2)

2 ➡️ be aware of the need for grammatical agreement in speech and writing, matching verbs to nouns/pronouns correctly. (Y2T2/3)

Before you start

Background knowledge

The term 'collective noun' refers to nouns which identify a group of people, animals or objects, e.g.

a crowd (people)
a herd (sheep/cows/elephants)
a bunch (grapes/bananas/keys)

Resources for Session 1

Copymaster 38 Collective noun crossword

Resources for Session 2

Copymaster 39 Collective nouns

Assessment indicators

- Can the children identify collective nouns?
- Can they match collective nouns and verbs correctly?

Teaching the sessions

Session 1 ❶

Introduction `15-20 min`

▦ Begin by recapping on what the children understand by the term 'noun'. Ask for examples of common and proper nouns.

Explain to the children that you are going to look at another type of noun. Write 'collective noun' on the board and ask the children what they think a 'collective noun' might be.

Can they give you any examples?

If none of the children has ever come across the term before, write the following on the board:

a collection or group of:

people living in the same house and related	(family)
birds	(flock)
bananas	(bunch)

Can the children supply the words in brackets? Can they now define what a collective noun is? Can they help you to compile a list of common collective nouns?

Ask the children how using collective nouns makes their writing more interesting, i.e. it avoids having to repeat expressions such as 'a lot of' or 'a group of'.

A collective noun crossword `20-25 min`

👥 Give each pair **Copymaster 38 A collective noun crossword**. Some children may be unfamiliar with the way crosswords work, so you will need to be on hand to explain how to fill in the answers. 'Gaggle of geese' will probably be unfamiliar to the children, and their first thought for 'trees' may be 'wood'. Point out that each dash in the clue represents a letter in the word they are looking for.

Summary `10 min`

▦ Compare crossword answers through class discussion so that each pair can complete their crossword.

Using collective nouns `10-15 min`

👤 Each child should choose at least three of the answers in the crossword and put each in a sentence of their own.

Homework

Ask the children to make a list of other collective nouns. They should have at least five in their list.

Session 2 ②

Introduction 15-20min

▓ Start this session by investigating the lists of collective nouns the children have compiled at home. Write interesting/unusual examples on the board.
Taking each example in turn, ask the children to make sentences containing each collective noun. Some children may quite naturally use the singular form of verbs, e.g.

The orchestra was playing.

The army is marching.

However, because these nouns refer to more than one thing, some children will want to use plural forms of verbs, e.g.

The orchestra were ...

The army are ...

Bring in the children's knowledge of pronouns here. Ask:

Would we replace 'the orchestra' with he/she/it/they/I?

The children should realise that they would say 'it' and that therefore they would need to say 'it was'/'it is', etc.

Do this oral activity several times, reminding the children to think of the collective noun as 'it'.

Our own collective nouns 20min

⚫ Children can have fun devising their own collective nouns. You will need to be on hand to get them started as they often find it difficult to decide on groups of things to name. When they have devised at least three collective nouns, ask each group to use their new words in sentences.

Collective nouns 15-20min

▣ Each child should complete **Copymaster 39 Collective nouns**, which reinforces the idea that collective nouns make for more interesting writing, and allows you to assess whether the children have grasped noun/verb agreement for collective nouns.

A collective noun crossword

Complete this crossword. Remember, each dash in the clue represents a letter in the word you are looking for.

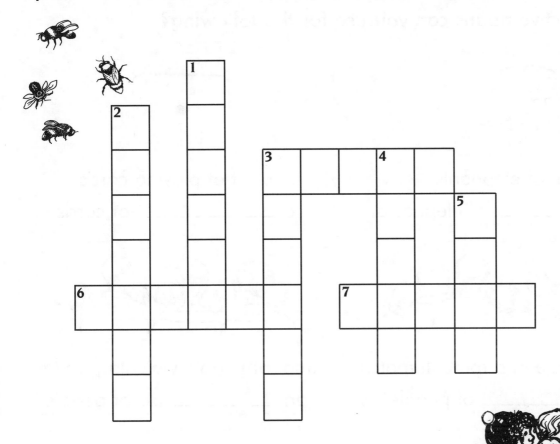

Across

3 a __ __ __ __ __ of sheep

6 a __ __ __ __ __ __ __ of geese

7 a __ __ __ __ __ of bees

Down

1 a __ __ __ __ __ __ of beads

2 a __ __ __ __ __ __ __ __ of books

3 a __ __ __ __ __ __ of trees

4 a __ __ __ __ __ of people

5 a __ __ __ __ of cows

Collective nouns

Using collective nouns means we don't have to keep writing 'a lot of' or 'a group of'.

Which collective nouns can you use for the following?

a lot of elephants

a _____ of elephants

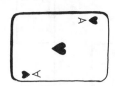

a lot of playing cards

a _____ of cards

a lot of people at a football match

a _____ of people

a lot of people watching a play

an _____ of people

a group of stars

a _____ of stars

a lot of grapes on one stalk

a _____ of grapes

Use each of these collective nouns in sentences of your own.

_____

_____

_____

_____

_____

_____

UNIT 3 | Abstract nouns

Learning target

On completion of this unit the children should be able to:

1 ➤➤ identify and use abstract nouns. (Y5/T2)

Before you start

Background knowledge

Defining abstract nouns is not as straightforward as defining common and proper nouns. A working definition that most children can grasp is that an abstract noun is the name of something you cannot touch, see, taste, hear or smell.

Most abstract nouns fall into the following categories:

Qualities:	wisdom/cowardice, etc.
Feelings:	jealousy/sadness, etc.
Times:	morning/Friday, etc.

Resources for Session 1

Copymaster 40 Which type of noun?

Copymaster 41 Using abstract nouns

Assessment indicators

- Can the children identify abstract nouns?
- Can they use abstract nouns in their own writing?

Teaching the session

Session 1 ①

Introduction 20-25 min

▨ By now the children should be comfortable with the concept of what a noun is. Recap on what they know by writing the following headings on the board and asking for examples:

common nouns proper nouns collective nouns

Explain that there is another category of nouns which are called 'abstract nouns'. These nouns are words we use for qualities, feelings and times, amongst other things.

Take each of these areas in turn and investigate them with the children:

Qualities: These can be 'good' or 'bad' and can relate to people, animals and objects, e.g.

the bravery of the young man
the fierceness of the tiger
the roughness of the tree trunk

Feelings: Again, these can be 'good' or 'bad'. They usually relate to people but can be used for animals, especially when animals appear as characters in stories, e.g.

the happiness of the girl
the misery of the lost child

the anger of the wounded lion
the sorrow of the red hen

Times: Abstract nouns of time can refer to periods of time, days, months, etc. You can also point out that some abstract nouns are also proper nouns. Examples of abstract nouns are 'the summer', 'August', 'last month', 'this year'.

Write the above lists on the board as you explain. Can the children add any more abstract nouns to each list?

Which type of noun? 15-20 min

⁛ Ask each group to complete a copy of **Copymaster 40 Which type of noun?** The 'abstract noun' column is the most difficult so you may need to prompt the children to ask questions to help with the categorisation, e.g.

Can we touch/see it?
Is this the name of how we can feel?

Summary 10 min

▨ The groups can compare how they have categorised the nouns through class discussion. Spend some time investigating any nouns which have been wrongly categorised.

Using abstract nouns 15-20 min

▤ Each child should complete **Copymaster 41 Using abstract nouns**, which gives the opportunity to use abstract nouns in the context of sentence writing.

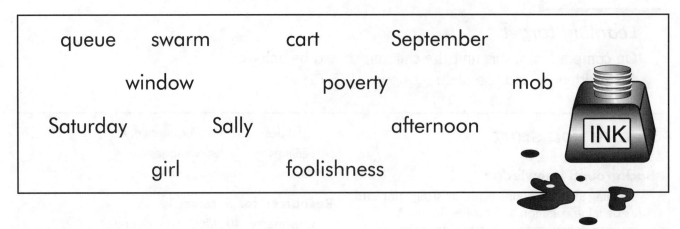

queue   swarm   cart   September

window   poverty   mob

Saturday   Sally   afternoon

girl   foolishness

Look at the nouns in the box.

Decide which type of noun each one is and write it in the correct list.

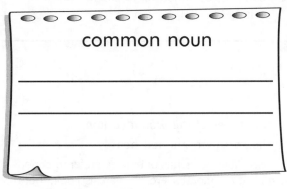

common noun

_____

_____

_____

proper noun

_____

_____

_____

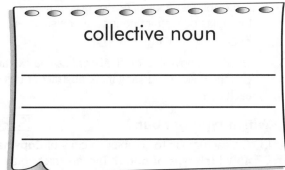

collective noun

_____

_____

_____

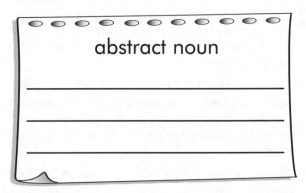

abstract noun

_____

_____

_____

Use one of the nouns from each list in sentences of your own.

_____

_____

_____

_____

_____

_____

A Use the correct abstract noun from the box to complete each sentence.

> friendship   freedom   kindness   morning

1 I caught the train early in the _____ .

2 The _____ between Frank and Kim had ended with a quarrel.

3 "You have shown great _____ to this wounded dog," said the vet.

4 "In two years I will have my _____!" shouted the slave.

B Use each of these abstract nouns in sentences of your own.

> fear   robbery   pleasure   evening

_____

_____

_____

_____

_____

_____

_____

_____

UNIT 4 | Compound nouns

Learning target

On completion of this unit the children should be able to:

1 ➡️ identify and use compound nouns. (Y5T2)

Before you start

Background knowledge

A compound word is defined by the Concise Oxford Dictionary as 'a word made up of two or more existing words'. For the purposes of this unit, the definition is a noun made up of two other nouns, e.g. 'matchbox', 'doorstep'.

There is an added complication that some compound nouns are hyphenated, so have a comprehensive dictionary with you at all times to check!

Resources for Session 1

Copymaster 42 Snowy and watery words

Copymaster 43 Making and using compound nouns

Assessment indicators

- Can the children identify compound nouns?
- Can they make compound nouns from a given list of words?

Teaching the session

Session 1 ①

Introduction [10-15 min]

As with other units in this section, begin by recapping on what the children understand by the term 'noun' and give them the opportunity to suggest nouns for the following categories:

    common nouns
    proper nouns
    collective nouns
    abstract nouns

Explain to the children that there is one more type of noun which completes the family, i.e. compound nouns. These are, quite simply, nouns which are made up by joining two other nouns together, e.g. 'spaceship', 'snowman', 'bookcase'.

Can the children add any more to the list?

Snowy and watery words [10-15 min]

Give each group **Copymaster 42 Snowy and watery words**. Allow the children to use dictionaries if they want to.

Summary [10 min]

Compare the children's compound noun lists through class discussion. Typical answers could include:

snow
snowball / snowdrift / snowdrop / snowflake / snowline / snowman / snowplough / snowshoe / snowstorm

water
waterbed / waterbird / watercolour / watercress / waterfall / waterfront / waterhole / waterline / watermark / watermelon / watermill / waterside / waterway / waterwheel

Making and using compound nouns [15-20 min]

Give each child **Copymaster 43 Making and using compound nouns** to complete.

Homework

The children should devise picture sums for at least five compound nouns.

Snowy and watery words

Write a compound noun beginning with **snow** by each snowflake.

* snow _____

* snow _____

* snow _____

* snow _____

* snow _____

* snow _____

* snow _____

* snow _____

Write a compound noun beginning with **water** on each droplet.

water _____

water _____

water _____

water _____

water _____

water _____

water _____

A What are these compound nouns?

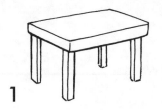

1 + = _____

 +

2 + = _____

3 + = _____

4 +  = _____

B Use each of the 4 compound nouns you have made in sentences of your own.

_____

_____

_____

_____

_____

_____

Making plurals

Write the plurals of these nouns.

wolf		lady	
woman		foot	
mosquito		pen	
scarf		cross	
donkey		goose	
wineglass		hero	
piano		pastry	
penny		cliff	
table		picture	
box		pony	
dictionary		loaf	
cabinet		child	
shelf		envelope	
fox		tooth	
potato		baby	
bus		tomato	
alley		journey	
servant		class	
man		match	
person		ox	
volcano		echo	

Categorising nouns

Put each of these nouns in the correct list.

cup	Wednesday	path	Australia	River Thames
raindrop	skylark	bundle	staircase	grief
coat	generosity	hatred	July	gang
moonlight	horse	skill	Scotland	crew
chorus	morning	team	postman	basket

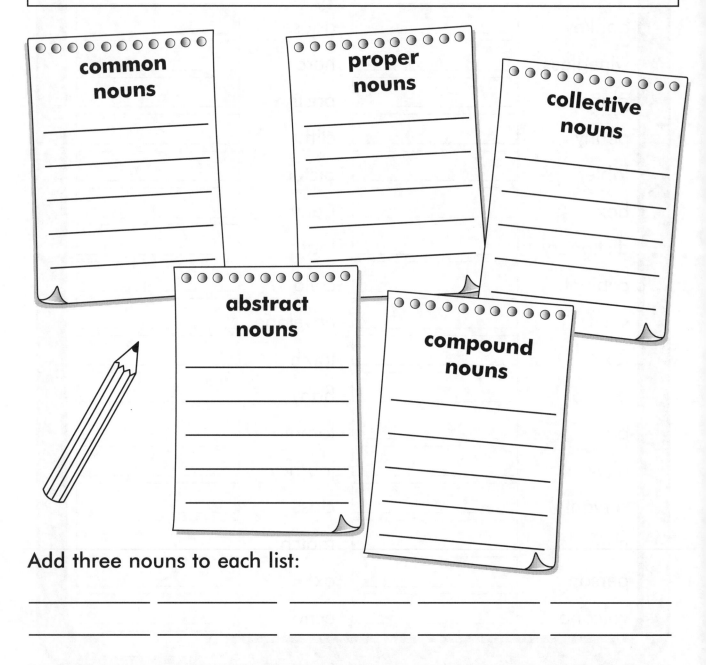

common nouns

proper nouns

collective nouns

abstract nouns

compound nouns

Add three nouns to each list:

PRONOUNS

Focus

The Units in this section look at the use of personal pronouns and possessive pronouns which stand in place of nouns. Relative pronouns are introduced but the work on clauses is investigated in depth in Section 7: Adjectives, Section 9: Adverbs and Section 10: Sentences.

Contents

Unit 1: Personal pronouns

Unit 2: Possessive pronouns

Unit 3: Relative pronouns

Assessment

At the end of this section children should be able to:

1 identify pronouns and understand their function in sentences

2 recognise the gender and number of pronouns

3 substitute pronouns for common and proper nouns in their own writing

4 ensure grammatical agreement of pronouns and verbs in speech and writing.

Assessment copymasters

The pronouns assessment copymasters are on pages 89–90.

Copymaster 54 Possessive pronouns gives the children the opportunity to identify and use possessive pronouns.

Copymaster 55 Relative pronouns gives the children the opportunity to use relative pronouns to form more interesting sentences and to join short sentences.

UNIT 1 | Personal pronouns

Learning targets

On completion of this unit the children should be able to:

1 ➤➤ be aware of the need for grammatical agreement in speech and writing, matching verbs to nouns/pronouns correctly, e.g. I am, the children are (Y3T2/Y5T2)

2 ➤➤ identify pronouns and understand their functions in sentences through noticing in speech and writing how they stand in place of nouns (Y3T3)

3 ➤➤ substitute pronouns for common and proper nouns in own writing (Y3T3)

4 ➤➤ distinguish the 1st, 2nd and 3rd person forms of pronouns, e.g. I, me, we, you, she, her, them (Y3T3)

5 ➤➤ investigate how pronouns are used to mark gender, e.g. he, she, etc. (Y3T3)

Before you start

Background knowledge

This unit introduces the children to personal pronouns, which can be used in place of nouns, and investigates number and gender.

Resources for Session 1

Copymaster 46 The Jones family

Copymaster 47 Using pronouns

Resources for Session 2

Copymaster 48 Verb/pronoun agreement

Assessment indicators

- Can the children recognise personal pronouns?
- Can they use pronouns in their own writing?

Teaching the sessions

Session 1 ② ③ ④ ⑤

Introduction 20-30min

▨ Begin by recapping on what the children understand by the term 'noun' and introduce them to the term 'pronoun' meaning a word which stands in place of a noun.

Write the following examples on the board:

Mary is walking to school. — She is walking to school.

Tom is fishing. — He is fishing.

The children are playing. — They are playing.

Investigate how Mary/she, Tom/he and children/they correspond; i.e. they refer to the same thing/person.

Do some oral practice with the class. Ask the children to suggest sentences which include the name(s) of the children in the class, e.g.

Sally is wearing a blue jumper.

Christopher has broken his pencil.

How could the children say these sentences without using the children's name? i.e.

She is wearing a blue jumper.

He has broken his pencil.

Ask the children what pronoun someone would use to refer to:

himself/herself? What is special about this pronoun?	(I)
two people including himself/herself?	(we)
a dog?	(it)
the person sitting next to them?	(he/she)
three people, not including themselves?	(they)

Spend some time investigating number and gender of pronouns. The children will be familiar with the terms 'singular' and 'plural'. Ask them to help you compile a list of pronouns which refer to one person or thing and a list which refers to more than one person or thing, e.g.

Singular	Plural
I	we
me	us
myself	ourselves
you	you
yourself	yourselves
he	they
him	
himself	
she	them
her	
herself	
it	themselves
itself	

Look at the lists with the children and investigate which pronouns can only be used for females, which for males and which can be used for either depending on who/what is being referred to.

The Jones family
`20-25 min`

 Put the children in small groups and give each group **Copymaster 46 The Jones family**. They are required to write a short description of each member of the family without repeating their names. Discuss with the children the sorts of things they might write about, e.g. size, age, hair, clothes, etc. They can be as imaginative as they like! They should underline the pronouns they use.

Summary
`10 min`

 Compare the descriptions through class discussion, listing the pronouns used on the board.

Using pronouns
`15 min`

 Give each child **Copymaster 47 Using pronouns**. For Section B, encourage the children to write interesting sentences.

Homework

The children can finish the copymaster for homework.

They can look for examples of pronouns in their reading books.

Session 2

Introduction
`20 min`

 Use this short session to recap on what the children understand by the term 'pronoun' and to check that they understand the need for verb/pronoun agreement. Remind the children of the work they did on verbs and tenses in Key Stage 1. If you feel they are unsure at this point, revise the work from *Learning Targets: Grammar and Punctuation Key Stage* 1, Section 5.

As most of the grammatical errors in this context centre on the verb 'to be', ask the children to help you compile verb tables for the past, present and future tenses using pronouns, i.e.

Past

I was	we were
you were	you were
he was	they were
she was	
it was	

Present

I am	we are
you are	you are
he is	they are
she is	
it is	

Future

I shall	we shall
you will	you will
he will	they will
she will	
it will	

Pronoun/verb agreement
`15 min`

Copymaster 48 Pronoun/verb agreement will highlight any areas of confusion which the children may have.

Write a description of each member of the family. Do not repeat their names – use pronouns instead.

Mum _____

_____

_____

_____

Dad _____

_____

_____

_____

Becky _____

_____

_____

_____

_____

Sam _____

_____

_____

_____

Patch _____

_____

_____

_____

Using pronouns

A Choose the correct pronoun to replace the bold words.

it	she
him	
he	they

1   The children played with the kite and **the kite** got stuck in the tree.

_____

2   We told the boys that **the boys** could play with the ball.

_____

3   The goalkeeper said that the ball had whizzed by
the goalkeeper.

_____

4   Sara wanted to go out so **Sara** put her coat on.

_____

5   Ali rode his bicycle and **Ali** had a puncture.

_____

B   Use these pronouns in sentences of your own.

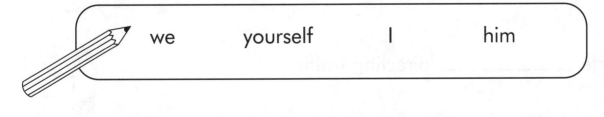

we	yourself	I	him

_____

_____

_____

_____

A Use **is** or **are** to complete each sentence.

1 They _____ covered in snow.

2 It _____ digging for a bone.

3 She _____ skipping.

4 He _____ reading.

5 We _____ twins.

B Use **was** or **were** to complete each sentence.

1 They _____ fighting.

2 It _____ broken.

3 She _____ sitting down.

4 He _____ directing traffic.

5 We _____ lost.

UNIT 2 Possessive pronouns

Learning target

On completion of this unit the children should be able to:

1 ➡➤ distinguish between personal pronouns, e.g. I, you, him, it, and possessive pronouns, e.g. mine, yours, hers. (Y3T3)

Before you start

Background knowledge

The main difficulty with possessive pronouns is distinguishing them from possessive adjectives. The latter stand in front of a noun, e.g.

> her book
> my coat
> your letter

whereas, possessive pronouns do not, e.g.

> The book is hers.
> The coat is mine.
> The letter is yours.

'His' is both a possessive pronoun and a possessive adjective, e.g.

> his dog
> The dog is his.

Resources for Session 1

Copymaster 49 Which possessive pronoun?

Copymaster 50 Using possessive pronouns

Assessment indicators

- Can the children recognise possessive pronouns?
- Can they use possessive pronouns in their own writing?

Teaching the session

Session 1   ①

Introduction   20–30 min

▦ Recap on what the children understand by the term 'pronoun', i.e. a word that can be used in place of a noun. Ask for examples.

Explain that there is a special group of pronouns called 'possessive pronouns'. Can the children guess what they think possessive pronouns might do in a sentence? It may help to remind them of the apostrophe of possession.

Once you have established that possessive pronouns signal that something is 'owned' (possessed), write the following on the board:

> This house is <u>my house</u>.   (mine)
> This coat is <u>your coat</u>.   (yours)
> This dog is <u>her dog</u>.   (hers)

Ask the children if there is a way of writing these sentences which avoids repeating the nouns 'house', 'coat' and 'dog' respectively. Stress that repeating words in writing often makes it dull to read. We use personal pronouns to avoid having to repeat people's names, etc. and we also use possessive pronouns to avoid repetition.

Which possessive pronoun?   10–15 min

⚉ Give each group **Copymaster 49 Which possessive pronoun?** The Copymaster is structured in such a way that only using a possessive pronoun, rather than a possessive adjective, will make sense in each case.

Summary   10 min

▦ Compare the answers through group discussion. Can the children see what happens to 'your', 'her', 'our', 'their' to make possessive pronouns? (add 's')

Using possessive pronouns   20 min

👤 **Copymaster 50 Using possessive pronouns** gives the children further practice.

Homework

The children can complete the copymaster for homework.

They can look for examples of possessive pronouns in their reading books.

Which possessive pronoun?

Rewrite each sentence using a possessive pronoun instead of repeating the noun. The first one is done for you.

1   That bicycle is my bicycle.

That bicycle is mine.

2   These books are your books.

3   The black pen is his black pen.

4   Those shoes are her shoes.

5   These bags are our bags.

6   Those dogs are their dogs.

Using possessive pronouns

Write a sentence which includes both possessive pronouns.

his   mine

_____

_____

yours   hers

_____

_____

mine   theirs

_____

_____

theirs   ours

_____

_____

ours   his

_____

_____

UNIT 3 | Relative pronouns

Learning targets

On completion of this unit the children should be able to:

1 ➤➤ identify pronouns and understand their functions in sentences (Y3T3)

2 ➤➤ ensure that, in using pronouns, it is clear to what or whom they refer. (Y5T2)

Before you start

Background knowledge

The relative pronouns which the children will need to use most frequently are 'who', 'which' and 'that'. They have two functions in sentences:

- they stand in place of a noun
- they act as conjunctions and are related to the noun which comes immediately before them, e.g.

  The tree just missed the man who was chopping it down.

  The dog ran in front of the bus which was turning the corner.

'Who' is always used for people.

'Which' and 'that' are used for animals and objects.

A common mistake with relative pronouns is using them in such a way as to make them refer to the wrong noun, e.g.

  The taxi hit the lamppost, which was going too fast.

This sounds as if the lamppost was going too fast! It should be written either as

The lamppost was hit by the taxi, which was going too fast.

or

The taxi, which was going too fast, hit the lamppost.

NB The concepts of defining and non-defining relative clauses are not discussed in this book as they are too complex for children at this stage. The rules governing which relative pronoun to use have also been kept simple in line with the NLS requirements for this level.

Resources for Session 1

Copymaster 51 Who or which? (1)

Copymaster 52 Who or which ? (2)

Resources for Session 2

Copymaster 53 What does it mean?

Assessment indicators

- Can the children consistently use 'who' relating to people and 'which/that' relating to animals and objects.
- Can the children use 'who', 'which'/'that' as conjunctions?

Teaching the sessions

Session 1 ①

Introduction 20-30min

▓ Recap on what the children understand by the term 'pronoun'. Ask for examples of personal and possessive pronouns. Suggest some personal and possessive pronouns and ask the children to give you sentences in which they are used.

Explain that you are now going to investigate one further group of pronouns called 'relative pronouns'. They are very useful words because they stand in place of a noun and can be used as conjunctions. Ensure the children understand the term 'conjunction' and remind them of their Key Stage 1 work on

'and', 'but', 'because' and 'then'. If they seem at all unsure at this point, spend some time revising these conjunctions (*Learning Targets: Grammar and Punctuation Key Stage 1*, Section 7).

Write 'who' and 'which' on the board, explaining that these are the most common relative pronouns. You may want to introduce 'that' at this point and it is sufficient to tell the children that 'that' and 'which' do the same job.

Complete the information on the board by adding:

who = people   which = animals and
                    (that)   objects

Work through several examples on the board, e.g.

> The man washed the dog.
> The dog was dirty.

Ask if these two sentences should be joined by 'who' or 'which', i.e.

> The man washed the dog, which was dirty.

Ask the children to tell you the noun 'which' is replacing, i.e. the dog.

Other examples:

> The cat scratched the man.
> The man was teasing it.
> The cat scratched the man, who was teasing it.
>
> We went to the park.
> The park had a slide.
> We went to the park, which had a slide.

Point out that relative pronouns, like other pronouns, make a piece of writing more interesting to read because, by using them, you can avoid repetition and too many very short sentences.

'Who' or 'which'? (1) | 15 min

Give each pair **Copymaster 51 Who or which? (1)**. Some children will find this difficult so be on hand to guide them by asking:

> Which noun are you going to replace with a relative pronoun?
>
> Is the noun a person, animal or object?

Summary | 10 min

Compare answers through class discussion. To clarify the concept for any children who are still unsure, write several examples from the copymaster on the board and bracket the noun you do not want to repeat.

> I have a sister.
> (My sister) lives in Australia.

Is the noun a person? Use 'who'.
Is the noun an animal? Use 'which'.
Is the noun an object? Use 'which'.

> I have a sister who lives in Australia.

Who or which? (2) | 15-20 min

Copymaster 52 Who or Which? (2) gives the children further practice in using relative pronouns.

Homework

The children can complete Copymaster 52 for homework.

They can look for examples in their reading books of sentences with the relative pronouns 'who' and 'which'.

Session 2

Introduction | 15-20 min

Use this short session to show the children that it is very important to use relative pronouns correctly or the meaning of a sentence can be muddled.
Write the following example on the board:

> The leopard climbed the tree, which was injured.

Ask the children what information the sentence is giving. They will probably tell you that the injured leopard climbed a tree. Investigate the sentence carefully to see that it actually says that the leopard climbed the injured tree! Ask the children how they could rearrange the words so it says what it should:

> The tree was climbed by the leopard, which was injured.
>
> The leopard, which was injured, climbed the tree.

The second example is by far the most elegant but the commas surrounding the clause 'which was injured' are an added complication here. Concentrate on the children grasping the relationship between the relative pronoun and the noun to which it refers. Work on commas and clauses dealt with in Section 7: Adjectives and Section 9: Adverbs.

Investigate further examples of sentences that need re-arranging before the children tackle the group work, e.g.

> The patient was treated kindly by the nurse who had a broken leg.
>
> The flowers grew well in the tubs which had spiky leaves.

What does it mean? | 20 min

Copymaster 53 What does it mean? requires the children to reorder the words in each sentence, establishing the correct relative pronoun/noun relationship so that the sentence makes sense. They must also make up a sentence of their own which doesn't say exactly what it is meant to.

Summary | 10-15 min

Compare the answers to A through class discussion. Those groups which have attempted B should write their sentences on the board for the rest of the class to sort out.

85

51 | Who or which? (1)

Join these pairs of sentences with **who** or **which**.

1 I have a sister.
My sister lives in Australia.

_____

2 Harry bought a football.
The football was red and white.

_____

3 I lost the pen.
The pen was a gift from my brother.

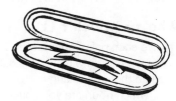

_____

4 Peter had a book.
The book was about Ancient Greece.

_____

5 I am going to visit my uncle.
My uncle lives on a farm.

_____

6 We have our holidays in a caravan.
The caravan is by the sea.

_____

52 | Who or which? (2)

A Use **who** or **which** to complete these sentences.

1 I have a letter _____ has come all the way from America.

2 Have you seen the new family _____ moved in next door?

3 The book _____ I am reading is very exciting.

4 We helped the old lady _____ had hurt her leg.

5 I baked a cake _____ everyone said was delicious.

B

1 Write a sentence of your own using **who** as a conjunction.

_____

_____

2 Write a sentence of your own using **which** as a conjunction.

_____

_____

A Sort out the sentences so they say what they mean.

1 The dog chased the rabbit which was called Rover.

_____

2 My friend has a baby brother who lives next door.

_____

3 The old car skidded into the gate which had a flat tyre.

_____

4 The apple fell off the tree which was ripe.

_____

5 The child said hello to the teacher who was playing on the climbing frame.

_____

B Make up a sentence of your own which doesn't quite say what it should. Can your friends sort it out?

_____

_____

_____

Possessive pronouns

A Underline the possessive pronoun in each sentence.

1 "That pen is mine," said Paul.

2 "Which coat is yours?" asked the teacher.

3 "These bicycles are ours," claimed the twins.

B Copy the sentences. Use a possessive pronoun instead of the underlined words.

1 Your brother is taller than <u>my brother</u>.

_____

2 I have found a ruler. Is it <u>your ruler</u>?

_____

3 There are some bags on the floor. Are they <u>your bags</u>?

_____

4 Her work is neater than <u>his work</u>.

_____

C 1 Write a sentence using the possessive pronoun **ours**.

_____

_____

2 Write a sentence using the possessive pronoun **hers**.

_____

_____

A Write **who** or **which** to complete each sentence.

1 The doctor looked after the little girl _____ had fallen off her bicycle.

2 The farmer milked the cows _____ he had brought in from the field.

3 The runner polished his medal _____ he had won on Saturday.

4 My cousin sent me a birthday present _____ she had bought in Spain.

5 I wrote a letter to my friend _____ I am going to visit in the summer.

B Rewrite these sentences so they say what they actually mean!

1 The cup fell off the draining board which was made of china.

_____

_____

2 The horse jumped over the fence which was called Silver.

_____

_____

3 The old book was put on the shelf which was torn.

_____

_____

ADJECTIVES

Focus

The National Literacy Strategy introduces adjectives in Y3T2, but simple adjectives are introduced in *Learning Targets: Grammar and Punctuation Key Stage* 1, Section 4, as children will meet 'describing words' in their early reading books and will attempt to use them at this early stage in their own writing.

The units in this section cover revision of the Key Stage 1 work, expanding the range of adjectives and investigating impact, and progress to adjectives of degree, adjectival phrases and adjectival clauses.

Contents

Unit 1: Simple adjectives – revision and extension of Key Stage 1 work

Unit 2: Adjectives of degree

Unit 3: Adjectival phrases and clauses

Assessment

At the end of this section children should be able to:

1 identify and use simple adjectives

2 identify and use adjectives to express degree

3 identify and use adjectival phrases and clauses.

Assessment copymasters

The assessment copymasters are on pages 108–109.

Copymaster 66 Adjectives of degree gives the children the opportunity to form and use comparative and superlative adjectives.

Copymaster 67 Adjectival phrases and clauses gives the children the opportunity to use adjectival phrases and clauses in descriptive writing.

Simple adjectives

Learning targets

On completion of this unit the children should be able to:

1 ➤➤ identify adjectives in shared reading (Y3T2)

2 ➤➤ collect and classify adjectives, e.g. for colours, sizes, moods (Y3T2)

3 ➤➤ experiment with deleting and substituting adjectives and note the effect on meaning (Y3T2)

4 ➤➤ experiment with the impact of different adjectives through shared writing. (Y3T2)

Before you start

Background knowledge

The sessions in this unit concentrate on helping the children to identify adjectives and to use them to improve their own writing. Building on this revision of Key Stage 1 work, the children are given the opportunity to extend their range of adjectives through thesaurus work.

Resources for Session 1

Copymaster 56 An adjective alphabet

Copymaster 57 Interesting adjectives

Copymaster 58 Adjectives

Resources for Session 2

Copymaster 59 Choosing adjectives

simple thesauruses

Assessment indicators

- Can the children identify and use simple adjectives?

- Can they improve their writing by adding and substituting adjectives?

Teaching the sessions

Session 1 ① ②

Introduction   20min

 Begin by asking the children to suggest some everyday nouns. Select those which will give the best opportunity for descriptive work and write them on the board as follows:

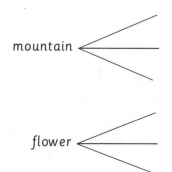

Ask the children what is meant by a describing word. Can they remember the correct term (i.e. 'adjective')? Ask them to suggest adjectives to describe the nouns on the board so you can complete an adjective 'fan' for each noun, e.g.

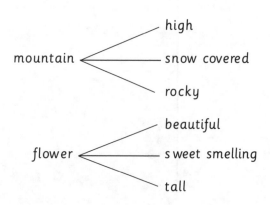

Ensure the children understand that colours and numbers are also adjectives by asking them to complete the following sentences:

number   colour
adjective   adjective

_____ birds sat on a _____ tree.

_____ women wore _____ hats.

_____ boys had _____ hair

If necessary do/repeat Adjectives Unit 2 from *Learning Targets Key Stage* 1: *Grammar and Punctuation*.

An adjective alphabet   `15-20min`

Give each group **Copymaster 56 An adjective alphabet** to complete. Be on hand to check work in progress and to suggest that the children think of more interesting adjectives than 'nice', 'big', etc. The children will find some of the letters, e.g. 'x', 'z', impossible, so draw the activity to a close when the groups have completed most of the copymaster. Keep these copymasters for use in later adjective units.

Summary   `10min`

It would be quite time-consuming to ask each group for every adjective so either:

- ask group 1 for an adjective beginning with 'a', group 2 for 'b', and so on.

or

- ask which group thinks they have a really interesting adjective for 'a', 'b', and so on.

Interesting adjectives   `15-20min`

Each child should complete **Copymaster 57 Interesting adjectives** by writing three more interesting adjectives for each of the over-used adjectives given. Encourage the use of simple thesauruses to help them.

Homework

Copymaster 58 Adjectives gives the children the opportunity to identify adjectives in sentences, and to complete sentences by adding interesting adjectives.

Session 2   ③ ④

Introduction   `20-30min`

Recap on what the children understand by the term 'adjective'. Ask for examples.

Explain that using adjectives makes a piece of writing more interesting. Write the following on the board:

The enormous crocodile opened its huge mouth to show its sharp, pointed teeth.

Ask the children to identify each adjective and, as they do, put a thin line through each one. Ask the children to read the sentence with the adjectives and then without the adjectives. Investigate the differences. Which do they consider the more interesting

sentence? Which sentence gives them more information? Which sentence makes it easier to see the crocodile in their imagination?

Write several more 'bald' sentences on the board and ask the children to add adjectives to improve them, e.g.

The dog found a bone.

My kite got stuck in the tree.

The boy read a book.

Once the children have grasped that adjectives carry interest and information, progress to looking at the choice of adjectives. Write sentences with common, over-used adjectives on the board, e.g.

My big dog frightened the nice postman.

The old man lived in a little house.

Ask the children to identify the adjectives in each sentence and then to replace them with adjectives which give the reader a much clearer picture, e.g.

big – enormous/massive/gigantic

nice – friendly/helpful/cheerful

old – ancient/doddery/elderly

little – tiny/cramped

Choosing adjectives   `15-20min`

Copymaster 59 Choosing adjectives allows the children to experiment with using adjectives to create a given response in a reader. Be on hand to ensure that the children have understood the required 'response'.

Summary   `10min`

Compare the groups' sentences through class discussion, stressing that choosing adjectives carefully has a direct impact on how a reader responds to a piece of writing.

Using a thesaurus   `15-20min`

Ask the children to copy this list of adjectives from the board:

pale   dark
bad   cold

Using a simple thesaurus, they should compile a list of adjectives that could be substituted for each adjective on the list. They should then choose their favourite for each one and use it in a sentence of their own.

Possible substitutes:

pale – white/colourless/light/sallow/ashen/ pallid

bad – evil/wicked/mean/faulty/harmful/rotten

dark – black/dim/shady/unlit/murky/ebony

cold – cool/chilly/frosty/icy/wintry/arctic

Homework

The children can complete the copymaster for homework.

An adjective alphabet

For each letter of the alphabet, write an adjective which begins with that letter.

a _____   b _____   c _____

d _____   e _____   f _____

g _____   h _____   i _____

j _____   k _____   l _____

m _____   n _____   o _____

p _____   q _____   r _____

s _____   t _____   u _____

v _____   w _____   x _____

y _____   z _____

Interesting adjectives

For each adjective in bold, write three adjectives which mean the same, or nearly the same. Choose interesting adjectives.

a **big** mountain _____ _____ _____

a **little** insect _____ _____ _____

a **pretty** dress _____ _____ _____

a **good** book _____ _____ _____

a **sad** film _____ _____ _____

an **unhappy** child _____ _____ _____

a **happy** child _____ _____ _____

a **bad** storm _____ _____ _____

58 | **Adjectives**

A Underline all the adjectives in each sentence.

1 A massive boulder fell onto the narrow road.

2 Seven bicycles were chained to the iron gate.

3 The small boat was tossed about on the rough sea.

4 Five dusty books were found on the bottom shelf.

5 The sleek panther ran through the tall grass.

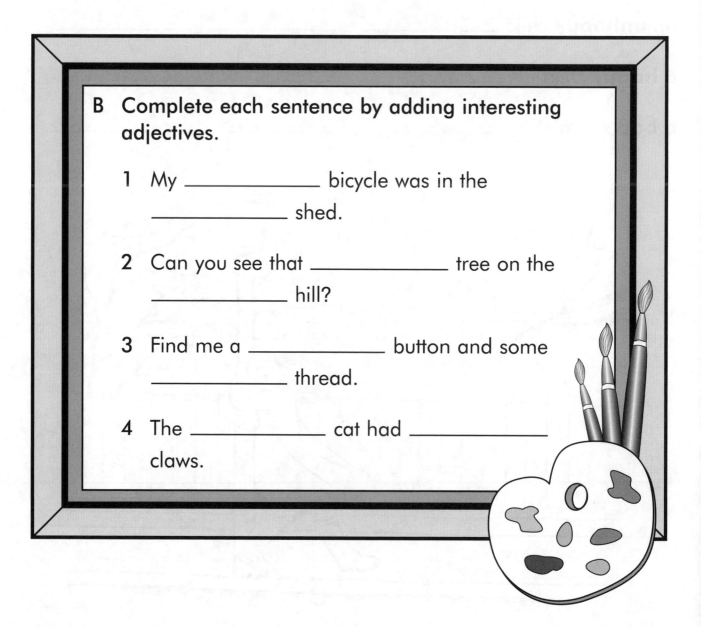

B Complete each sentence by adding interesting adjectives.

1 My _____ bicycle was in the _____ shed.

2 Can you see that _____ tree on the _____ hill?

3 Find me a _____ button and some _____ thread.

4 The _____ cat had _____ claws.

1 To complete these sentences choose adjectives that will make your reader frightened.

The _____ man rode up to the _____ castle.

The _____ drawbridge came down slowly and a

_____ ghost floated across to meet him.

2 Choose adjectives to complete these sentences that will make your reader feel safe and happy.

The _____ man rode up to the _____ castle.

The _____ drawbridge came down slowly and a

_____ ghost floated across to meet him.

3 Choose adjectives to complete these sentences that will make your reader laugh.

The _____ man rode up to the _____ castle.

The _____ drawbridge came down slowly and a

_____ ghost floated across to meet him.

UNIT 2 | Adjectives of degree

Learning targets

On completion of this unit the children should be able to:

1 ➤➤ identify and use adjectives on a scale of intensity, e.g. 'hot', 'warm', 'tepid', 'lukewarm', 'chilly', 'cold' (Y4T2)

2 ➤➤ identify and use comparative and superlative adjectives (Y4T2)

3 ➤➤ relate adjectives of degree to suffixes which indicate degrees of intensity, e.g. '-er', '-est' [Y4T2]

4 ➤➤ relate adjectives of intensity to adverbs which indicate degrees of intensity, e.g. 'very', 'quite', 'more', 'most'. (Y4T2)

Before you start

Background knowledge

Adjectives can show degrees of intensity in three main ways:

1 through a list of adjectives showing ascending or descending intensity, e.g. 'hot', 'warm', 'tepid', etc.

2 through use of the comparative and superlative forms, e.g. 'hot', 'hotter', 'hottest'

3 through the addition of adverbs, e.g. 'very quiet', 'quite small', 'rather loud', etc.

'More' and 'most' in front of some adjectives form their comparative and superlative, e.g. 'frightening', 'more frightening', 'most frightening'.

Resources for Session 1

Copymaster 60 How dark? How light?

simple thesauruses

Resources for Session 2

Copymaster 56 An adjective alphabet – new copies and the ones the children have previously completed

Copymaster 61 Making comparisons

Assessment indicators

- Can the children recognise and use adjectives of intensity?

- Can they form and use comparatives and superlatives?

- Can they identify adverb/adjective phrases to show degrees of intensity?

Teaching the sessions

Session 1 ①

Introduction `20 min`

▓ Begin by recapping on what the children understand by the term 'adjective'. Ask for examples.

Write 'hot' and 'cold' on the board and ask the children to help you compile a word web of adjectives with similar meanings. Give the children the context of 'weather' which will help them to focus on suitable adjectives. The finished webs may look something like the diagram opposite.

Adjectives of degree `15 – 20 min`

◉ The next stage can be done as group work. Ask the children to make the word webs into two lists. A list of 'hot' words beginning with the least hot and working up to the hottest, and a list of 'cold' words

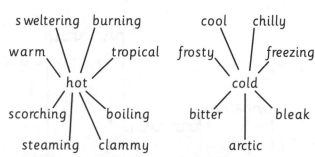

beginning with the least cold and working up to the coldest. Bear in mind that some subjective judgment will be exercised as the children compile their lists, for example 'scorching' is obviously hotter than 'warm' but ordering 'burning', 'tropical', 'steaming', etc. is more subjective.

Summary `10 – 15 min`

▓ Compare the lists and ask the children to justify their choices. The importance of this activity is not that they produce a 'correct' list, but that they extend their vocabulary and appreciate that carefully chosen adjectives will enhance their writing. To this end, discuss with the children why we need so many words for 'hot' and 'cold'. Why are those two words not always sufficient to convey what we want to say?

How dark? How light? `20-25 min`

Give each child **Copymaster 60 How dark? How light?**, which repeats the class/group activities with the adjectives 'dark' and 'light'.

Homework

The children can choose three of their interesting 'dark' words and three interesting 'light' words to use in sentences of their own.

Session 2

Introduction `20-30 min`

Recap on Session 1, explaining that the adjectives they have been investigating can be used for comparing things, e.g.

The weather was warm yesterday but it is scorching today.

It was cold last night, but it is freezing this morning.

Explain that adjectives can be used in another way for comparisons.

Comparative adjectives are used when we want to compare two things. We usually add 'er' to the adjective to form the comparative, e.g.

This water is hot.

That water is hotter.

Write a list of adjectives and their comparative forms on the board and investigate how they are formed and any spelling changes, e.g.

warm	warmer
kind	kinder
sad	sadder
cool	cooler
happy	happier
windy	windier
wide	wider

Point out that if an adjective already ends in 'e' we just add 'r'.

Look at 'long' adjectives, for example 'frightening', 'important', 'gracious' etc., and explain that 'frighteninger', 'importanter', etc. are awkward to say, so adjectives like these form their comparatives with the word 'more', e.g.

more frightening

more important

more gracious

more fantastic

more attractive

Go on to explain the rules for comparing three or more things, i.e. adding 'est'. Write a list of adjectives and their superlatives on the board and investigate how they are formed and any spelling changes, e.g.

short	shortest
long	longest
fine	finest
hot	hottest
sleepy	sleepiest

Point out that if an adjective already ends in 'e' we just add 'st'.

Look at the 'long' adjectives, 'frightening', etc. again. These adjectives form their superlatives with 'most', e.g.

most frightening

most important

most gracious

Comparative and superlative adjective alphabet `25-30 min`

Give each group Copymaster 56 which they completed for Unit 1, and another, clean copy. The children should write the heading 'Comparatives and Superlatives' on the new copy. Taking each adjective in turn from their original adjective alphabet, the children should write the comparative and superlative forms on their new sheet.

Summary `10-15 min`

Compare answers through class discussion. Check spelling as well as form.

Making comparisons `15 min`

Copymaster 61 Making comparisons gives the children the opportunity to use and form comparative and superlative adjectives.

Homework

The children can produce a list of five adjectives which form their comparatives and superlatives with 'er'/'est', and five which form them with 'more'/'most', e.g.

adjective	comparative	superlative
bright	brighter	brightest
famous	more famous	most famous

They should copy and learn the irregular comparatives and superlatives as follows:

adjective	comparative	superlative
bad	worse	worst
good	better	best
little	less	least
much	more	most
many	more	most
some	more	most

How dark? How light?

A Use a thesaurus to complete the word webs. You can add more lines if you wish.

dark

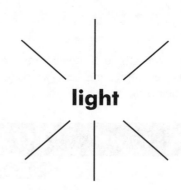

light

B Put your words in a list, beginning with the least dark.

Put your words in a list, beginning with the least light.

A Use the comparative or superlative form of the adjective in bold to complete each sentence.

1 **lazy**   John is _____ than Harry.

2 **cloudy**   Tuesday was the _____ day this week.

3 **heavy**   That suitcase is _____ than this one.

4 **young**   I am the _____ one in my family.

5 **sad**   That was the _____ day of my life.

B Finish the chart.

adjective	comparative	superlative
brown		
dangerous		
short		

C Use these comparative and superlative adjectives in sentences of your own.

most peaceful _____

_____

sunnier _____

_____

loudest _____

_____

Adjectival phrases and clauses

Learning targets

On completion of this unit the children should be able to:

1 ➡➡ construct adjectival phrases (Y4T2)

2 ➡➡ construct adjectival clauses. (Y5T2)

Before you start

Background knowledge

Adjectival phrases and clauses are both groups of words that cannot stand alone and make sense. A phrase is a group of words without a verb, and a clause is a group of words with a verb.

An adjectival phrase can be used to enhance the description of something, e.g.

The dog <u>with the injured paw</u> was taken to the vet.

The crowd was <u>noisy and excited</u> when the match began.

<u>Ten large white</u> boxes were delivered yesterday.

An adjectival clause tells us more about a noun or pronoun in the main clause. Both the main clause and the adjectival clause have verbs but the main clause can stand alone and make sense whereas the adjectival clause cannot, e.g.

We went to the park <u>which had swings</u>.

Main clause = We went to the park

Adjectival clause = which had swings

Adjectival clauses begin with 'who', 'which' or 'that'.

'Who' is used for people, e.g.

I knew the boy <u>who had broken the window</u>.

'Which' and 'that' are used for animals and objects, e.g.

The police found the car <u>which had been stolen</u>.

Sometimes adjectival clauses split the main clause and are marked with commas, e.g.

The tree, <u>which had been battered by the storm</u>, was cut down.

Main clause = The tree was cut down

Adjectival clause = which had been battered by the storm

Resources for Session 1

Copymaster 62 Find the adjectival phrase

Copymaster 63 Using adjectival phrases

Resources for Session 2

Copymaster 64 Find the adjectival clause

Copymaster 65 Using adjectival clauses

Assessment indicators

- Can the children identify and use adjectival phrases?
- Can they identify and use adjectival clauses?

Teaching the sessions

Session 1 ❶

Introduction 20-30 min

▨ Recap on what the children understand by the term 'adjective'. Ask for examples, revising colour, number, degree, etc.

Explain that we sometimes need more than one word to describe a noun or a pronoun and so we can use adjectival phrases. An adjectival phrase is a group of words without a verb which tells us more about a noun or pronoun.

Write the following examples from 'Before you start' on the board:

1 The dog <u>with the injured paw</u> was taken to the vet.

2 The crowd was <u>noisy and excited</u> when the match began.

3 <u>Ten large white</u> boxes were delivered yesterday.

Investigate how each adjectival phrase is formed to give the children models for their own writing:

1 adjectival phrase begins 'with …'
2 adjectival phrase is two adjectives joined by a conjunction
3 adjectival phrase is more than one adjective in front of the noun.

Practise the various ways of forming adjectival phrases through cloze procedure on the board, e.g.

The man with ＿＿＿＿＿＿＿＿＿ was crossing the road.
My dog was ＿＿＿＿＿ and ＿＿＿＿＿ when I came home.
＿＿＿ ＿＿＿ ＿＿＿ bushes were growing in our garden.

Find the adjectival phrase `15min`

Give each group **Copymaster 62 Find the adjectival phrase**. The children should discuss each sentence in turn and underline/highlight/circle each adjectival phrase.

Summary `10-15 min`

Compare answers through class discussion. Can the children substitute their own phrases for the ones they have picked out?

Using adjectival phrases `20-25min`

Copymaster 63 Using adjectival phrases gives the children the opportunity to use given adjectival phrases in sentences of their own, and to write adjectival phrases to describe a given list of nouns.

Homework

The children can complete the copymaster for homework.

They can write a short description, which must contain at least three adjectival phrases on a subject of their/your choice.

Session 2 ②

Introduction `25-30 min`

Recap on adjectival phrases, asking the children to define the term 'phrase' and give examples.

Explain that there are other groups of words, called adjectival clauses, which we use to describe things. An adjectival clause is a group of words with a verb and which begins with 'who', 'which' or 'that'.

Write the following examples from 'Before you start' on the board:

1 We went to the park <u>which had swings</u>.
2 I knew the boy <u>who had broken the window</u>.
3 The tree, <u>which had been battered by the storm</u>, was cut down.

Investigate how each adjectival clause is formed to give the children a model for their own writing:

1 adjectival clause beginning with 'which' and telling us more about the park
2 adjectival clause beginning with 'who' and telling us more about the boy
3 adjectival clause beginning with 'which' and placed in the middle of the sentence and marked with commas

Practise the various ways of forming adjectival clauses through cloze procedure on the board, e.g.

The zoo keepers caught the lion which ＿＿＿＿＿＿.

I walked to school with Tim, who ＿＿＿＿＿＿.

The bus, which ＿＿＿＿＿＿ , had broken down.

Find the adjectival clause `15min`

Give each group **Copymaster 64 Find the adjectival clause**. The children should discuss each sentence in turn and underline/highlight/circle each adjectival clause.

Summary `10-15 min`

Compare answers through class discussion. Can the children substitute their own clauses for the ones they have picked out?

Using adjectival clauses `20min`

Copymaster 65 Using adjectival clauses gives the children the opportunity to use given adjectival clauses in sentences of their own, and to write adjectival clauses to describe a given list of nouns.

Homework

The children can complete the copymaster for homework.

They can write a short description, which must contain at least three adjectival clauses, on a subject of their/your choice.

Ring the adjectival phrase in each sentence.

1   The boat was blue and white when we had finished painting it.

2   The lady with the umbrella is my aunty.

3   I found an old rusty coin in the garden.

4   Eight graceful white swans glided down the river.

5   The cave was dark and frightening.

6   The boy with the black hair scored the goal.

7   We have four small rabbits.

8   Lucy found a bird with a broken wing.

A Use these adjectival phrases in sentences of your own.

1 with an unhappy smile

_____

_____

2 steep and dangerous

_____

_____

3 two enormous green

_____

_____

B Write a sentence with an adjectival phrase for each of these nouns.

1 garage

_____

_____

2 tractor

_____

_____

3 doctor

_____

_____

adjectival
phases

Find the adjectival clause

Find the adjectival clause in each sentence.

1 We walked along the street which was silent and deserted.

2 The old shed, which hadn't been used for years, was to be our new den.

3 Chris picked the puppy which had a black patch over one eye.

4 The swimming instructor was pleased with the girl who had won the race.

5 I found my pencil which I had lost yesterday.

6 My uncle Joe, who is seventy years old, is coming to visit us.

7 Simon shouted at his brother who had punctured the bicycle.

8 The football match, which was a cup tie, was very exciting.

Using adjectival clauses

A Use these adjectival clauses in sentences of your own.

1 who hates playing football

_____

_____

2 which is next to the post office

_____

_____

3 , who was new to the job,

_____

_____

B Write a sentence with an adjectival clause for each of these nouns.

1 friend

_____

_____

2 computer

_____

_____

3 city

_____

_____

A Complete the following chart:

adjective	comparative	superlative
high	_____	_____
easy	_____	_____
soft	_____	_____
amazing	_____	_____
small	_____	_____
busy	_____	_____
nervous	_____	_____
little	_____	_____

B Write sentences using these adjectives:

1 the comparative of 'merry'

_____

2 the superlative of 'wise'

_____

3 the superlative of 'good'

_____

4 the superlative of 'beautiful'

_____

5 the comparative of 'sad'

_____

Choose one of the following and write a description. You must include at least 2 adjectival phrases and 2 adjectival clauses in your description and underline them.

sports day

the jungle

the river

VERBS

Focus

Learning Targets: Grammar and Punctuation Key Stage 1 introduces the children to verbs and the simple past, present and future tenses.

The work at Key Stage 2 is somewhat more complicated and you should take every opportunity, through shared and guided reading, to investigate interesting verbs, to discuss tenses and how they are formed, and to alert the children to the impact of powerful verbs.

The units in this section cover the impact of verbs on reader response, auxiliary verbs, and active and passive verbs.

Contents

Unit 1: Powerful verbs

Unit 2: Auxiliary verbs

Unit 3: Active and passive verbs

Assessment

At the end of this section children should be able to:

1 select appropriate verbs to enhance their writing

2 use various forms of the auxiliary verbs 'to be' and 'to have' in order to accurately convey 'time' in their writing

3 use the active and passive form of verbs appropriately.

Assessment copymasters

The assessment copymasters are on pages 127–128.

Copymaster 78a The break-in is a piece of continuous prose for the children to read.

Copymaster 78b Verbs asks the children to investigate, identify and substitute verbs in the passage on Copymaster 78a. They are also required to continue the story and underline the verbs they use.

UNIT 1 | Powerful verbs

Learning targets

On completion of this unit the children should be able to:

1 ➤➤ collect and classify examples of verbs from reading and own knowledge, e.g. 'run', 'chase', 'sprint'; 'eat', 'consume', 'gobble'; 'said', 'whispered', 'shrieked' (Y3T1)

2 ➤➤ experiment with changing simple verbs in sentences and discuss their impact on meaning (Y3T1)

3 ➤➤ identify the use of powerful verbs, eg 'hobbled' instead of 'went', through cloze procedure. (Y4T1)

Before you start

Background knowledge

The sessions in this unit will help children to realise the wide variety of verbs open to them to use in their writing. They will also have the opportunity of substituting verbs in sentences in order to convey meaning more accurately and be introduced to the idea of reader response.

Resources for Session 1

Copymaster 68 How do we do that?

Copymaster 69 Classifying verbs

large sheets of paper

Resources for Session 2

Copymaster 70 How would I walk if ...?

Copymaster 71 Using powerful verbs

Assessment indicators

- Can the children classify verbs according to meaning?

- Can they select verbs which accurately convey meaning?

Teaching the sessions

Session 1 ❶

Introduction $\boxed{20-30\,\text{min}}$

▨ Recap on what the children understand by the term 'verb'. If necessary, use *Learning Targets: Grammar and Punctuation Key Stage* 1, Section 5 to revise verbs and simple tenses.

As this unit concentrates on the selection of verbs to enhance the children's writing, introduce them to the idea of a verb family with a family name, for example 'to walk' (infinitive), to avoid them suggesting verbs in a variety of tenses.

Ask for examples of verb family names. Select those which come from at least two groups and write them on the board randomly, e.g.

> to say   to run   to sprint   to whisper
>
>   to walk   to jump   to shout

Ask the children to help you to classify the verbs, e.g.

ways we speak	*ways we move*
to say	to walk
to whisper	to sprint
to shout	to jump
	to run

Whatever the categories of verbs you have on the board, ask the children to add to the lists. Can they think of unusual/interesting verbs?

How do we do that? $\boxed{15\,\text{min}}$

▟ **Copymaster 68 How do we do that?** requires the children to write groups of verbs which are related to one type of action/activity. Encourage them to discuss the verbs they think of, select the most interesting and write them in the infinitive (to ...), i.e. the family name.

Summary `10 min`

Discuss the verb categories with the children. If time permits, let them vote on the 'best' verbs and list them on the board.

Classifying verbs `20 min`

Copymaster 69 Classifying verbs gives the children the opportunity to work individually on classifying verbs and using some in their writing.

Homework

The children should make a note of any interesting verbs they find in their reading.

Pin a large piece of paper to a noticeboard in the classroom. The children can write the interesting verbs they find on individual slips of paper and stick them to the board.

Session 2 ② ③

Introduction `20 min`

Having focused the children's attention on the wide variety of verbs they could use in their own writing, this session brings in the idea of redrafting work to improve it.

Explain that it is difficult to hit on exactly the right word the very first time you write something. Reading your work through after you have finished gives you a chance to improve it. One of the ways to improve a piece of writing is to look at the choice of verbs.

Write the following sentences on the board:

The man _fell_ into the river.

My cat _climbed_ the tree.

Sally _smiled_ when she won the prize.

Ask the children to focus on the underlined verbs. Take each sentence in turn and ask the children to suggest other verbs they could use, e.g.

fell	_climbed_	_smiled_
to drop	to clamber	to grin
to sink	to scamper	to laugh
to slip	to ascend	to smirk
to tumble	to scale	to beam

Spend some time replacing the underlined verbs with the children's suggestions and investigate the impact on the reader, e.g.

The cat _climbed_ the tree.

The cat _scampered_ up the tree.

What difference does this make to the reader's picture of how the cat went up the tree?

How would I walk if ... `15 min`

Give each group **Copymaster 70 How would I walk if ...** The children should discuss each scenario and choose a verb which most accurately conveys how they would walk. They can choose more than one verb and use a thesaurus to help them.

Summary `10 min`

Write the list of verbs on the board as each group gives you their answer to reinforce the variety open to them. Take a vote on which verb is best for each scenario.

Using powerful verbs `20 min`

Give each child **Copymaster 71 Using powerful verbs**. They should complete the sentences in Section A with interesting verbs, and use the verbs in Section B in sentences of their own.

What verbs could you use instead of **to eat**?

What verbs could you use to show what people do in **a swimming pool**?

What verbs could you use to show how people **play football**?

What verbs could you use instead of **to laugh**?

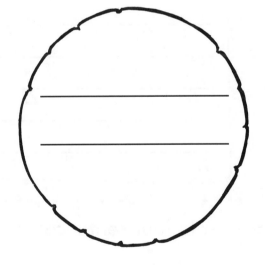

Classifying verbs

A Put the verbs in the correct list.

to write   to vacate

to quit   to sketch   to abandon

to draw   to jot   to forsake

to correspond   to desert   to withdraw

to doodle   to scribble   to depart

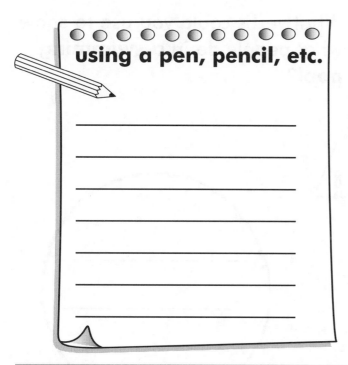

using a pen, pencil, etc.

**to leave someone
or somewhere**

B   Write four sentences. Use two words from each list.

How would I walk if ...

For each situation choose a verb that best describes how you would walk.

How would I walk if ...

1 I had a stone in my shoe?

_____

_____

2 I was in a hurry?

_____

_____

3 I was on parade in the army?

_____

_____

4 I was walking purposefully?

_____

_____

5 I had a lot of time to get where I was going?

_____

_____

6 I was out for exercise?

_____

_____

Using powerful verbs

A Complete the sentences using interesting verbs.

1 I _____ the kitten from the river.

2 I _____ out of school when
the bell went.

3 I _____ a moment before I went
into the room.

4 I _____ six red apples and some juicy strawberries.

B Use these interesting verbs in sentences of your own.

1 to scheme _____

_____

2 to organise _____

_____

3 to thrust _____

_____

4 to retreat _____

_____

UNIT 2 | Auxiliary verbs

Learning target

On completion of this unit the children should be able to:

1 ➡➡ investigate how different tenses are formed by using auxiliary verbs, e.g. 'have', 'was', 'shall', 'will'. (Y5T1)

Before you start

Background knowledge

Key Stage 1 work on verbs introduced the future tense, which is formed by using the future tense of the verb 'to be' as an auxiliary/helper verb, with an infinitive, e.g.

I shall go   you will go

The verb 'to be' and the verb 'to have' are used as auxiliary verbs to make verb tenses. For your information, the main tenses with which the children should be familiar are given in the chart below.

The chart shows the way the verbs are formed and it is entirely at the discretion of the teacher as to how much of the chart's information is imparted to the children.

The emphasis of the unit is that the children:

- are aware of how tenses are formed with auxiliary verbs
- can use the various tenses accurately in their writing.

Resources for Session 1

Copymaster 72 Identifying auxiliary verbs

Copymaster 73 Using auxiliary verbs

Resources for Session 2

Copymaster 74 Identifying and using auxiliary verbs

Assessment indicators

- Can the children identify auxiliary verbs?
- Can they use auxiliary verbs in their writing to accurately convey the timing of actions/events?

Tense	Example	Formation
simple present	I walk, you sing, they run	use of the infinitive without 'to be'
continuous present	I am walking, you are running	present tense of the verb 'to be' with present participle – 'ing'
simple past	I walked, you sang, they ran	past participle – 'ed'/irregular past participle
continuous past	I was walking, you were singing	past tense of verb 'to be' with present participle – 'ing'
perfect past	I have walked, you have sung	present tense of verb 'to have' with past participle – 'ed'/irregular
pluperfect	I had walked, you had sung	past tense of verb 'to have' with past participle – 'ed'/irregular
future	I shall walk, you will walk	future tense of verb 'to be' with infinitive

Teaching the sessions

Session 1   ②

Introduction   20-25 min

▓ Recap on what the children understand by the term 'verb'. Ask the children to give you examples using the verb family name, i.e. the infinitive, e.g.

to talk   to write   to read

Revise tenses from Key Stage 1 – present, past, future. Investigate how the future tense is formed:

verb 'to be' +	infinitive
I shall	laugh
you will	walk
he will	read
she will	play

it will	growl
we shall/will	watch
you will	write
they will	draw

Explain to the children that the verb 'to be' and the verb 'to have' are often used as auxiliary verbs.

Write the following list on the board:

I am	_____	I was	_____
You are	_____	You were	_____
He is	_____	They were	_____
I have	_____	I had	_____
You have	_____	You had	_____
She has	_____	We had	_____

Take each in turn and ask the children to supply another verb to complete the sentence, e.g.

I am walking.

You were running.

She has eaten.

We had finished.

Investigate how these verbs are formed and look at them in terms of the 'time' they convey. The children should be aware of the present/past distinction, but they should also be aware that 'had' signals an action further back in time, e.g.

She had finished her homework before she went out.

Identifying auxiliary verbs [15min]

Give each group **Copymaster 72 Identifying auxiliary verbs**. They should identify the auxiliary verbs by underlining them. Encourage the children to discuss each sentence in terms of the 'time' which the verb signals.

Summary [10min]

Answers can be compared through class discussion.

Using auxiliary verbs [15–20min]

Copymaster 73 Using auxiliary verbs gives the children the opportunity to complete sentences and use various tenses in sentences of their own. The sentences in Section A can be completed in either the present or past tense.

Homework

Ask the children to look through the book they are currently reading and find examples of sentences with auxiliary verbs.

Session 2

Introduction [20min]

Use this short session to investigate other auxiliary verbs i.e. 'could', 'should', 'would', 'might', 'must'. Auxiliary verbs in this group usually signal either a 'condition', i.e. where the action is dependent on something else, or the imperative, i.e. some degree of being ordered to do something.

Write an example of each on the board, e.g.

You could do the shopping for me.

I should do the shopping today.

We would do the shopping today.

She might do the shopping today.

They must do the shopping today.

Investigate how changing the auxiliary verb changes the intended meaning. How could the sentences be extended to make the meaning clear? For example:

You could do the shopping for me today if you would like to.

I should do the shopping today because we have no food.

We would do the shopping today if we weren't so busy.

She might do the shopping today if I ask her nicely.

You must do the shopping today because it is your turn.

Identifying and using auxiliary verbs [15–20min]

Give each child **Copymaster 74 Identifying and using auxiliary verbs** to work through.

Summary [10–15 min]

Compare answers through class discussion. In Section A, investigate how the sentences could be extended to make the meaning clearer or give extra information, e.g.

The curtains would fit the window in the other room if I took them up.

I might go swimming today if Dad will take me to the sports centre.

In Section B, investigate extending the children's sentences to make the meaning clearer or give extra information.

Underline the auxiliary verb in each sentence. Write **past**, **present** or **future** at the end of each sentence.

1 She was looking for her bag before she went to school.   _____

2 We shall plant more trees next month.   _____

3 The train had left the station before we arrived.   _____

4 The postman had delivered the letter to the wrong address.   _____

5 They are playing football in the park.   _____

6 The horses were galloping across the field.   _____

7 These houses were built over a hundred years ago.   _____

8 I have set the table for tea.   _____

A Use the auxiliary verbs **am**, **are**, **was** or **were** to fill the gaps.

1 The crows _____ flying around the garden.

2 I _____ hoping to go to town this afternoon.

3 You _____ looking in the wrong place.

4 The sheep _____ huddled in the corner of the field.

B Use these verbs in sentences of your own.

1 had walked

_____

_____

2 have given

_____

_____

3 were enjoying

_____

_____

4 will tidy

_____

_____

Identifying and using auxiliary verbs

A Underline the auxiliary verb in each sentence.

1 The curtains would fit the windows in the other room.

2 I might go swimming today.

3 Everyone must arrive at school by 8.45.

4 We should visit our friends in the holidays.

5 You could tidy the kitchen for me.

B Use these combinations of auxiliary verbs and verbs in sentences of your own.

1 could buy

_____

_____

2 should go

_____

_____

3 would try

_____

_____

4 must leave

_____

_____

Active and passive verbs

Learning targets

On completion of this unit the children should be able to:

1 ➤➤ understand the terms 'active' and 'passive' (Y6T1)

2 ➤➤ identify examples of active and passive verbs in texts (Y6T2)

3 ➤➤ experiment in transforming from active to passive and vice versa and study the impact of this on meaning. (Y6T2)

Before you start

Background knowledge

The children need to be comfortable with the concept of the subject and the object in sentences to be able to deal with the active and passive voice of verbs. Do the work in Section 10: Sentences – Unit 1 before you tackle this unit.

Every opportunity should be taken to investigate the uses of the active and passive voice in the children's own reading, the latter being found, predominantly, in information texts.

Resources for Session 1

Copymaster 75 Identifying active and passive verbs

Copymaster 76 Using active and passive verbs

Resources for Session 2

Copymaster 77 Changing active and passive verbs

Assessment indicators

- Can the children identify active and passive verbs?

- Can they transform active verbs to passive verbs and vice versa?

Teaching the sessions

Session 1 ① ②

Introduction `20-30 min`

▨ Revise 'subject' and 'object' in sentences. Write some simple sentences on the board and ask the children to identify the subject and the object in each case, e.g.

The snow covered the path.

  subject = snow   object = path

My dad bought a bicycle.

  subject = dad   object = bicycle

Explain to the children that when the action of the verb is done *by* the subject we say the verb is 'active'.

Ask them for examples of simple sentences where the verb is being done by the subject. Write a selection on the board and annotate them as follows:

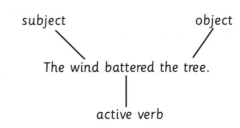

Use the children as 'living' examples, e.g.

Sam is reading the book.

Sulim is writing a story.

Write some simple sentences on the board where the subject of the sentence has the action done *to* it and ask the children to identify the subject and the agent, e.g.

The cup was broken by the boy.

  subject = cup   agent = the boy
  (object in active   (subject in active
  sentence)   sentence)

The rabbit was chased by the dog.

subject = rabbit   agent = dog
(object in active   (subject in active
sentence)   sentence)

Explain to the children that when the action of the verb is done to the subject we say the verb is 'passive'.

Ask them for examples of simple sentences where the verb is being done to the subject. Write a selection on the board and annotate them as follows:

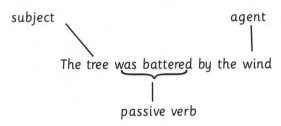

subject   agent

The tree was battered by the wind

passive verb

Use the children as 'living' examples, e.g.

The book is being read by Sam.
The story is being written by Sulim.

Identifying active and passive verbs |15min|

Give each group **Copymaster 75 Identifying active and passive verbs**. Explain to the children that they must:

1 look for the subject of the sentence
2 look for the verb
3 decide if the verb is being done by the subject (active) or to the subject (passive).

Summary |10min|

Compare answers through class discussion. Investigate any sentences which have caused particular problems by identifying the subject and asking: Is the subject doing anything? Is something being done to the subject?

Using active and passive verbs |20min|

Copymaster 76 Using active and passive verbs gives the children the opportunity to complete sentences with active and passive verbs and use them in sentences of their own.

Homework

Ask the children to find examples of active and passive verbs in the books they are currently reading.

Session 2   ③

Introduction |20min|

Recap on what the children understand by 'active' and 'passive' verbs. Ask for sentences with examples of each. Select several with active verbs and write them on the board:

My baby brother tore my book.
The milkman delivered the milk.

Show the children how to turn these 'active' sentences into 'passive' sentences, i.e.

My book was torn by my baby brother.
The milk was delivered by the milkman.

Investigate:

1 any word changes, e.g. 'tore'/'torn'
2 any word additions, e.g. 'was'
3 any alteration in word order.

Repeat this activity to transform 'passive' sentences into 'active' sentences, e.g.

The ironing was done by my dad.
My dad did the ironing.

Explain to the children that, very often, passive verbs are used in information books and sometimes the specific person or thing doing the action is not mentioned, e.g.

The mountain was climbed first in 1953 and again in 1972.

Changing active and passive verbs |15min|

Copymaster 77 Changing active and passive verbs gives the children the opportunity to transform active verbs into passive and vice versa.

Summary |10min|

Compare the answers through class discussion.

Homework

Ask the children to find three examples of sentences in their current reading book of verbs being used actively and three examples of verbs being used passively.

Identifying active and passive verbs

75

Underline the verb in each sentence.
Write **active** or **passive** at the end of each sentence.

1   The army surrounded the town.   _____

2   The youngest swimmer won the race.   _____

3   Our house was hit by lightning.   _____

4   The hunter wounded the lion.   _____

5   Your mirror was broken by the fall.   _____

6   The computer was set up by the technician.   _____

7   A clumsy waitress spilled the drink.   _____

8   The manager calmed the angry customer.   _____

9   The magician was booed by the audience.   _____

10   Two sheep dogs rounded up the sheep.   _____

A Complete these sentences with active verbs.

1 The clown _____ with four coloured balls.

2 My horse _____ over the ditch.

3 Harry _____ a picture.

B Complete these sentences with passive verbs.

1 The gate _____ by the car.

2 Our house _____ by the man next door.

3 Sally _____ by the other girls.

C Use these active and passive verbs in sentences of your own.

1 cleaned _____

_____

2 was opened _____

_____

3 was covered _____

_____

4 buried _____

_____

A Rewrite the following sentences, changing the active verb in each to a passive verb.

1 Our teacher marked our stories.

_____

2 The doctor called for an ambulance.

_____

3 The fisherman mended his boat.

_____

4 Several birds nested in the oak tree.

_____

B Rewrite the following sentences, changing the passive verb in each to an active verb.

1 The popular song was sung by the famous singer.

_____

2 The town was covered by ash from the volcano.

_____

3 Every day the castle was visited by the prince.

_____

4 A speeding motorist was stopped by the police.

_____

Mona could not believe what she was seeing! She had left the house that morning as she usually did. Everything was fine then.

After her day at work, she had come home to find the house had been broken into by robbers. The window had been hit with a brick and her jewellery was gone.

Mona was just about to telephone the police when a police car arrived at her gate. The policeman got out of the car and came over to her.

"Good evening," he said. "My name is PC White. I've come to tell you that your neighbour reported someone standing by your house. We caught him red-handed. We've got your jewellery and the thief was taken away by another policeman."

"Well, that's a relief!" said Mona. "All I have to do now is to get the window fixed."

_____

_____

_____

_____

_____

_____

_____

Read the passage on Copymaster 78a carefully.

1 Replace the underlined verbs with more interesting ones.

   a had <u>come</u> home

   b had been <u>hit</u>

   c her jewellery <u>taken</u>

   d <u>got</u> out of the car

   e <u>standing</u> by your house

   f she <u>said</u>

had _____ home

had been _____

her jewellery _____

_____ out of the car

_____ by your house

she _____

2 Copy out two sentences which have auxiliary verbs.

_____

_____

_____

3 Copy out a sentence with an active verb.

_____

_____

_____

4 Copy out a sentence with a passive verb.

_____

_____

_____

5 On Copymaster 78a, continue the story by explaining how Mona got the window fixed. Underline all the verbs you use.

ADVERBS

Focus

Children will be used to reading and using simple adverbs to describe actions but the range open to them will be limited. This section seeks to widen their adverb vocabulary and to encourage them to use a range of adverbs to enhance their writing.

The units in this section cover single adverbs showing how, when or where an action is performed, comparative and superlative adverbs, and adverbial phrases and clauses.

Contents

Unit 1: How, when, where adverbs

Unit 2: Adverbs of degree

Unit 3: Averbial phrases and clauses

Assessment

At the end of this section children should be able to:

1 identify and use simple adverbs

2 identify and use adverbs to express degree

3 identify and use adverbial phrases and clauses.

Assessment copymasters

The assessment copymasters are on pages 147–148.

Copymaster 90 Adverbs of degree gives the children the opportunity to use comparative and superlative adverbs.

Copymaster 91 Adverbial phrases and clauses gives the children the opportunity to use adverbial phrases and clauses in their writing.

UNIT 1 | How, when, where adverbs

Learning targets

On completion of this unit the children should be able to:

1 ➤➤ find examples, in fiction and non fiction, of words and phrases that link sentences, e.g. 'after', 'meanwhile', 'during', 'before', 'then', 'next', 'after a while' (Y3T3)

2 ➤➤ identify adverbs and understand their function in sentences through:

- identifying common adverbs with the suffix 'ly' and discussing their impact on the meaning of sentences
- noticing where they occur in sentences and how they are used to qualify the meaning of verbs
- using adverbs with greater discrimination in own writing. (Y4T1)

Before you start

Background knowledge

The sessions in this unit concentrate on helping the children to identify adverbs and to use them to improve their own writing. The children are given the opportunity to extend the range of adverbs open to them.

Resources for Session 1

Copymaster 79 An adverb alphabet

Copymaster 80 Interesting adverbs

Copymaster 81 Adverbs

Resources for Session 2

Copymaster 82 Choosing adverbs

simple thesauruses

Assessment indicators

- Can the children identify and use simple adverbs?
- Can they improve their writing through addition and substitution of adverbs?

Teaching the sessions

Session 1 ① ②

Introduction ⌊20min⌋

▨ Begin by asking the children to suggest some common everyday verbs and write them on the board as follows:

to shout	to read	to walk
to look	to eat	to laugh

Explain to the children that there is a group of words called adverbs which help us to understand:

- how verbs are done
- when verbs are done
- where verbs are done.

Take each verb in turn and ask the questions beginning with 'how', 'when' and 'where', e.g.

How can I shout?   loudly, angrily
When can I shout? today, often, later
Where can I shout? here, outside

Point out to the children that many adverbs that show 'how' things are done end in 'ly' and ask them for examples to write on the board, e.g.

slowly quickly wisely neatly excitedly

An adverb alphabet 15-20min

 Give each group **Copymaster 79 An adverb alphabet** to complete. Be on hand to check work in progress and to suggest that the children think of interesting adverbs. The children will find some of the letters (e.g. 'x', 'z') impossible, so draw the activity to a close when the groups have completed most of the copymaster.

Summary 10min

It would be quite time-consuming to ask each group for every adverb so either:

- ask group 1 for 'a', group 2 for 'b' and so on, or
- ask which group thinks they have a really interesting adverb for 'a', 'b', and so on.

Interesting adverbs 15-20min

Each child should complete **Copymaster 80 Interesting adverbs** by writing three adverbs that can be substituted for each of the adverbs given.

Homework

Copymaster 81 Adverbs gives the children the opportunity to identify adverbs in sentences, and to complete sentences by adding interesting adverbs which answer how, when or where.

Session 2 ① ②

Introduction 20-30min

Recap on what the children understand by the term 'adverb'. Ask for examples of how, when and where adverbs.

Explain that using adverbs makes a piece of writing more interesting. Write the following on the board:

The boy ran hurriedly out of the shop and waved excitedly to his friend.

Ask the children to identify each adverb and, as they do, put a thin line through each one. Ask the children to read the sentence with the adverbs and then without the adverbs. Investigate the differences. Which do they consider the more interesting sentence/the sentence which gives them more information/the sentence which makes it easier to imagine what the boy is doing?

Write several more 'bald' sentences on the board and ask the children to add adverbs to improve them, e.g.

The dog buried his bone.
The old man walked down the road.
The boy shouted to his friend.

Once the children have grasped that adverbs carry interest and information, progress to looking at the choice of adverbs. Write sentences with common adverbs on the board, e.g.

I walked quickly down the road.
She smiled happily at her friend.

Ask the children to identify the adverbs in each sentence and then to substitute them with adverbs which will give a clearer picture to the reader, e.g.

 quickly – hurriedly/rapidly/swiftly
 happily – joyfully/excitedly

Choosing adverbs 15-20min

Copymaster 82 Choosing adverbs allows the children to experiment with using adverbs to show the feelings of a character clearly to the reader.

Summary 10min

Compare the groups' sentences through class discussion, stressing that choosing adverbs carefully has a direct impact on how a reader responds to a piece of writing.

Using a thesaurus 15-20min

Ask the children to copy this list of adverbs from the board:

angrily
silently
neatly

Using a simple thesaurus, they should compile a list of adverbs that could be substituted for each adverb on the list. They should then choose their favourite for each one and use it in a sentence of their own.

Possible substitutes:

angrily – furiously/irritatedly/exasperatedly/ passionately

silently – noiselessly/soundlessly/calmly

neatly – tidily/orderly/elegantly

Homework

The children can complete the activity for homework.

An adverb alphabet

For each letter of the alphabet, write an adverb beginning with that letter.

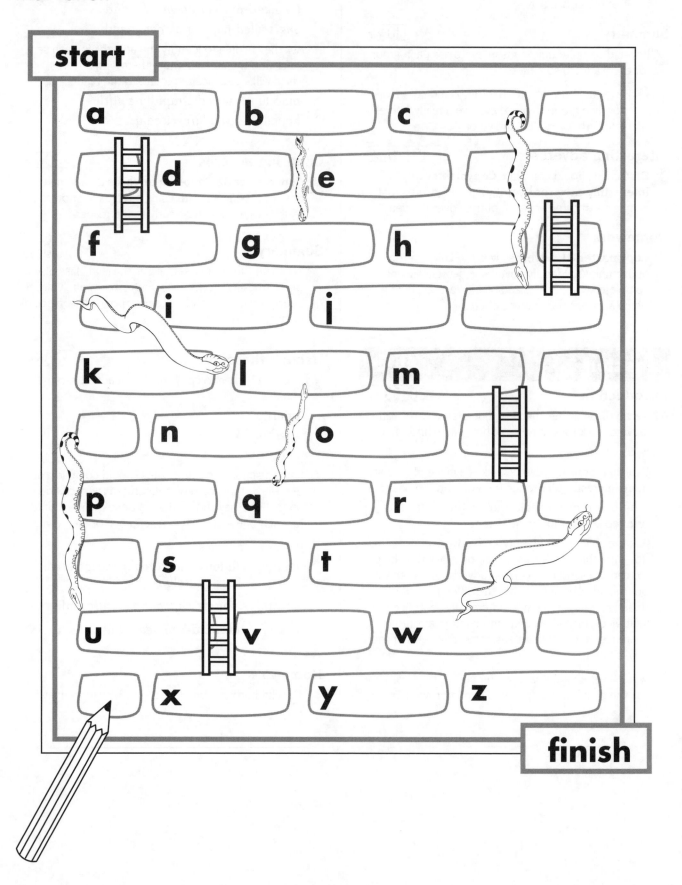

start

a   b   c

d   e

f   g   h

i   j

k   l   m

n   o

p   q   r

s   t

u   v   w

x   y   z

finish

Write three adverbs which you could use in place of the adverb in bold.

1   She answered **correctly**.

_____   _____   _____

2   He cried **unhappily**.

_____   _____   _____

3   The dog barked **loudly**.

_____   _____   _____

4   They argued **noisily**.

_____   _____   _____

5   The train arrived **late**.

_____   _____   _____

6   We looked **everywhere** for you.

_____   _____   _____

7   He put the cat **outside**.

_____   _____   _____

8   The letter was delivered **yesterday**.

_____   _____   _____

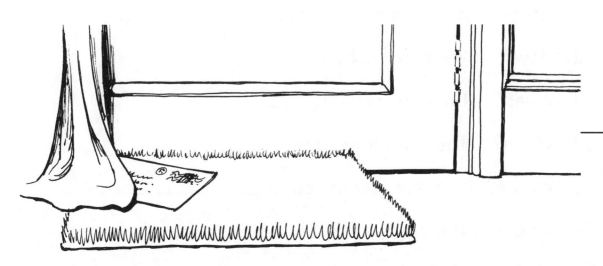

Adverbs

A Underline the adverbs in each sentence.

1 We looked for her everywhere.

2 The boy spoke respectfully to the policeman.

3 I always have cereal for my breakfast.

4 He often goes swimming.

5 I know I put the book here.

6 I broke the vase accidentally.

B Complete each sentence by adding an adverb to answer the question.

1 How?   Susan rides her bicycle _____.

2 How?   We play football _____.

3 When?   I will have my tea _____.

4 When?   They found the dog _____.

5 Where? I cannot find my book _____.

6 Where? The bag was left _____.

Choosing adverbs

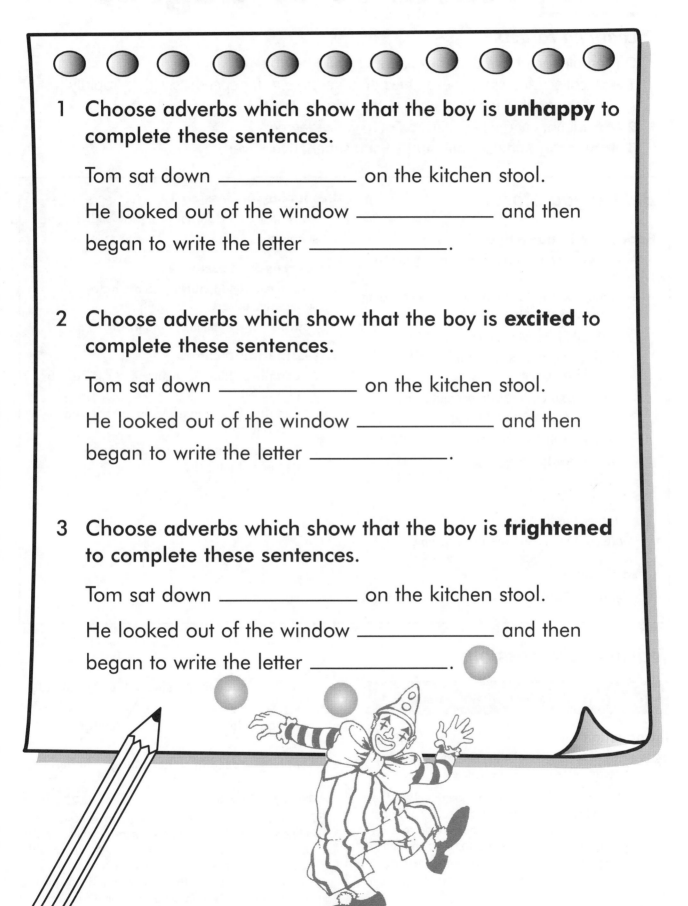

1 Choose adverbs which show that the boy is **unhappy** to complete these sentences.

Tom sat down _____ on the kitchen stool.

He looked out of the window _____ and then begin to write the letter _____.

He looked out of the window _____ and then began to write the letter _____.

2 Choose adverbs which show that the boy is **excited** to complete these sentences.

Tom sat down _____ on the kitchen stool.

He looked out of the window _____ and then began to write the letter _____.

3 Choose adverbs which show that the boy is **frightened** to complete these sentences.

Tom sat down _____ on the kitchen stool.

He looked out of the window _____ and then began to write the letter _____.

Adverbs of degree

Learning targets

On completion of this unit the children should be able to:

1 ➨ collect and classify examples of adverbs, e.g. for speed: 'swiftly', 'rapidly', 'sluggishly'; for light: 'brilliantly', 'dimly' (Y4T1)

2 ➨ identify and use adverb pairs to show degree

3 ➨ identify and use comparative and superlative adverbs.

Before you start

Background knowledge

Adverbs can show degrees of intensity in three main ways:

1 through a list of adverbs showing ascending or descending intensity, e.g.

sluggishly, slowly, quickly, rapidly

2 through use of the comparative and superlative forms, e.g.

quickly/more quickly/most quickly

3 through pairs of adverbs, e.g.

very quietly

quite heavily

more interestingly

most impressively

rather loudly

'More' and 'most' are the most common way of forming comparative and superlative adverbs, e.g.

clearly   more clearly   most clearly

Resources for Session 1

Copymaster 83 How happily? How sadly?

simple thesauruses

Resources for Session 2

Copymaster 84 Identifying comparative and superlative adverbs

Copymaster 85 Making comparisons

Assessment indicators

- Can the children recognise and use adverbs of intensity?
- Can they form and use comparatives and superlatives?
- Can they identify pairs of adverbs to show degrees of intensity?

Teaching the sessions

Session 1 ❶

Introduction 20min

▨ Begin by recapping on what the children understand by the term 'adverb'. Ask for examples.

Write 'quickly' and 'slowly' on the board and ask the children to help you compile a word web of adverbs with similar meanings. Give the children the context of 'walking', which will help them to focus on suitable adjectives. The finished webs may look something like this:

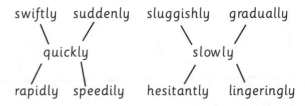

Adverbs of degree 15-20min

⚫⚫⚫ The next stage can be done as group work. Ask the children to make the word webs into two lists. A list of 'quick' words beginning with the least quick and working up to the quickest, and a list of 'slow' words beginning with the least slow and working up to the slowest. Bear in mind that some subjective judgement will be exercised as the children compile their lists.

Summary

10-15 min

Compare the lists and ask the children to justify their choices. The importance of this activity is not that they produce a 'correct' list, but that they extend their vocabulary and appreciate that carefully chosen adverbs will enhance their writing. To this end, discuss with the children why we need so many words for 'quickly' and 'slowly'. Why are these two words not always sufficient to convey what we want to say?

How happily? How sadly?

20-25 min

Give each child **Copymaster 83 How happily? How sadly?**, which repeats the class/group activities with the adjectives 'happily' and 'sadly'.

Homework

The children can choose three adverbs from each list from Copymaster 83 to use in sentences of their own.

Session 2

2 3

Introduction

20-30 min

Recap on Session 1, ensuring the children are comfortable with the concept of how, when and where adverbs.

Explain that adverbs can be used for comparisons. Comparative and superlative adverbs compare how something happens or is done in relation to how it happened on a different occasion, or how it was done by someone or something else.

We usually use the word 'more' in front of an adverb ending in 'ly' to form the comparative, e.g.

Sam exercised more vigorously than Tom.

Go on to explain the rules for superlative adverbs, i.e. these are formed by putting 'most' in front of adverbs which end in 'ly', e.g.

most interestingly	most sadly
most happily	most clearly

For adverbs which do not end in 'ly' the comparative is formed by adding 'er', and the superlative by adding 'est', e.g.

hard	harder	hardest
low	lower	lowest

Comparative and superlative adverbs

20-30 min

Give each group **Copymaster 84 Identifying comparative and superlative adjectives.** The children should discuss each sentence in turn and underline the comparative/superlative adverbs.

Summary

10-15 min

Compare answers through class discussion. Investigate whether the underlined adverbs are comparative or superlative.

Making comparisons

10-15 min

Copymaster 85 Making comparisons gives the children the opportunity to use and form comparative and superlative adverbs.

Homework

The children should learn the following irregular comparatives and superlatives:

well	better	best
badly	worse	worst

How happily? How sadly?

A Use a thesaurus to complete the word webs. You can add more lines if you wish.

happily

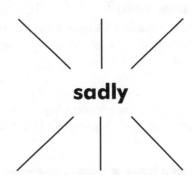

sadly

B Put your words in a list, beginning with the least happy.

Put your words in a list, beginning with the least sad.

Identifying comparative and superlative adverbs

Underline the comparative and superlative adverbs in each sentence.

1 Mr Brown waited most patiently until it was his turn.

2 I worked harder this term than I did last term.

3 She can play tennis more skilfully than her sister.

4 I feel better than I did yesterday.

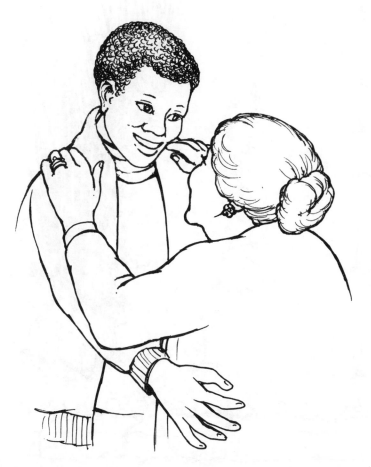

5 Sam arrived earlier than the others.

6 She spoke most clearly when it was her turn.

7 I have never known anyone behave more dishonestly.

8 You must come and visit more often.

Making comparisons

Use the comparative or superlative form of the adverb on the left to complete each sentence.

1 fairly   The competition was judged _____ than last year.

2 truthfully Of the three boys, Ali answered _____.

3 hard   I tried _____ than I did yesterday.

4 high   He jumped the _____ in the competition.

5 seriously   You have taken your work _____ than the others.

6 well   Those vegetables are growing _____ than these.

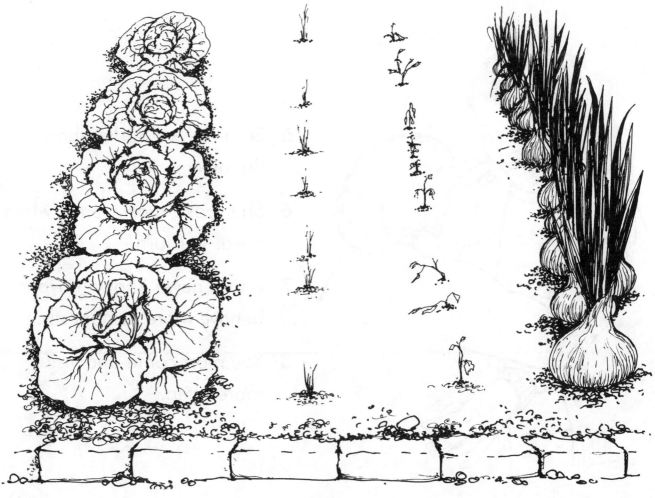

Adverbial phrases and clauses

Learning targets

On completion of this unit the children should be able to:

1 ➡ construct adverbial phrases (Y4T3)
2 ➡ construct adverbial clauses. (Y4T3)

Before you start

Background knowledge

As the children need to be comfortable with the term 'main clause', tackle this unit after Sentences: Unit 2.

Adverbial phrases and clauses are both groups of words that cannot stand alone and make sense. A phrase is a group of words without a verb, and a clause is a group of words with a verb.

An adverbial phrase can be used to enhance the description of how something happens/is done, e.g.

The car skidded to a halt <u>in a cloud of dust</u>.	(how)
The car skidded to a halt <u>at the last minute</u>.	(when)
The car skidded to a halt <u>near the edge of the cliff</u>.	(where)

An adverbial clause tells us more about the verb in the main clause. Both the main clause and the adverbial clause have verbs, but the main clause can stand alone and make sense whereas the adverbial clause cannot. Adverbial clauses begin with conjunctions, e.g.

The car skidded to a halt <u>because the tyre burst</u>.

Main clause = The car skidded to a halt

Adverbial clause = because the tyre burst

I will feed the dog <u>when I find the dog food</u>.

Main clause = I will feed the dog

Adverbial clause = when I find the dog food.

Resources for Session 1

Copymaster 86 Find the adverbial phrase
Copymaster 87 Using adverbial phrases

Resources for Session 2

Copymaster 88 Find the adverbial clause
Copymaster 89 Using adverbial clauses

Assessment indicators

- Can the children identify and use adverbial phrases?
- Can they identify and use adverbial clauses?

Teaching the sessions

Session 1 ①

Introduction 20-30 min

▦ Recap on what the children understand by the term 'adverb'. Ask for examples, revising how, when, where, degree, etc. Explain that we sometimes need more than one word to describe a verb and so we can use adverbial phrases. An adverbial phrase is a group of words without a verb which tells us more about the verb in the main clause.

Write the following examples from 'Before you start' on the board:

1 The car skidded to a halt <u>in a cloud of dust</u>.	(how)
2 The car skidded to a halt <u>at the last minute</u>.	(when)
3 The car skidded to a halt <u>near the edge of the cliff</u>.	(where)

Investigate how each adverbial phrase is formed and what information it gives so the children have models for their own writing:

1 adverbial phrase begins 'in …' and answers the question 'how?'.
2 adverbial phrase begins 'at …' and answers the question 'when?'.

3 adverbial phrase begins 'near …' and answers the question 'where?'.

Practise forming adverbial phrases to answer the questions how, when and where, on the board, e.g.

I went to the shops …	How?
I dug the garden …	When?
I found a pound coin …	Where?

Find the adverbial phrase   `15 min`

Give each group **Copymaster 86 Find the adverbial phrase.** The children should discuss each sentence in turn and underline/highlight/circle each adverbial phrase.

Summary   `10-15 min`

Compare answers through class discussion. Can the children substitute their own phrases for the ones they have picked out?

Using adverbial phrases   `20-25 min`

Copymaster 87 Using adverbial phrases gives the children the opportunity to use given adverbial phrases in sentences of their own, and write adverbial phrases to describe a given list of actions.

Homework

The children can complete the copymaster for homework.

They can write a short account of an event on a subject of their/your choice which must contain at least three adverbial phrases.

Session 2   ②

Introduction   `25-30 min`

Recap on adverbial phrases, asking the children to define the term 'phrase' and give examples.

Explain that there is another way of giving more information about the main verb, i.e. using adverbial clauses. An adverbial clause is a group of words with a verb and which begins with a conjunction, e.g. 'because', 'if', 'although', 'unless', 'even if', 'even though'.

Write the following examples on the board from 'Before you start':

> The car skidded to a halt <u>because the tyre burst.</u>
>
> I will feed the dog <u>when I find the dog food</u>.

Investigate how the adverbial clauses are formed and what information they give so the children have a model for their own writing:

1 adverbial clause begins with 'because' telling us why the car skidded.
2 adverbial clause begins with 'when' telling us when the dog will be fed.

Practise forming adverbial phrases, through cloze procedure on the board, e.g.

> We will catch the bus if
> _____.
>
> The dog chewed the jumper because
> _____.
>
> I don't want to go to the party even though
> _____.

Find the adverbial clause   `15 min`

Give each group **Copymaster 88 Find the adverbial clause**. The children should discuss each sentence in turn and underline/highlight/circle each adverbial phrase.

Summary   `10-15 min`

Compare answers through class discussion. Can the children substitute their own clauses for the ones they have picked out?

Using adverbial clauses   `20 min`

Copymaster 89 Using adverbial clauses gives the children the opportunity to use given adverbial clauses in sentences of their own, and to write adverbial clauses to describe a given list of verbs.

Homework

The children can complete the copymaster for homework.

They can write a short account on a subject of their/your choice which must contain at least three adverbial clauses.

Underline the adverbial phrase in each sentence.

1   An unexpected visitor arrived at our house late last night.

2   I left my bag outside the library.

3   I tidied my room in a hurry.

4   The branch snapped with a loud cracking noise.

5   She put her shoes in the cupboard.

6   He will be there in the afternoon.

7   The horse jumped the fence with great skill.

8   The team travelled to the match in the school bus.

A Use these adverbial phrases in sentences of your own.

1 from time to time _____

_____

2 without any noise _____

_____

3 at the bottom of the garden _____

_____

B Write a sentence with an adverbial phrase for each
of these verbs.

1 to scream _____

_____

2 to sleep _____

_____

3 to fly _____

_____

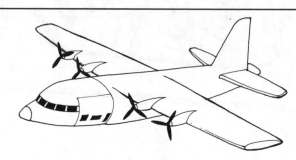

Find the adverbial clause

Underline the adverbial clause in each of these sentences.

1 He cannot ride his bicycle because it has a puncture.

2 We went for a swim when the rain had stopped.

3 They visited the zoo after they had their lunch.

4 No one is allowed in the room when my brother is playing the piano.

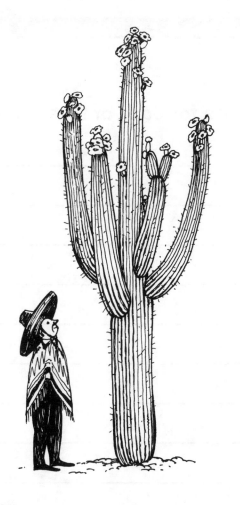

5 Meet me where the bus stop used to be.

6 The bird escaped because the cage door was left open.

7 You can go out to play if you wear your coat.

8 The flowers grew tall although no one watered them.

89 Using adverbial clauses

A Use these adverbial clauses in sentences of your own.

1 because the lock was broken

_____

_____

_____

2 even though I want to go

_____

_____

_____

3 although it hurts

_____

_____

_____

B Write a sentence with an adverbial clause for each of these verbs.

1 to try _____

_____

_____

2 to work _____

_____

_____

3 to obey _____

_____

_____

A Complete the chart.

adverb	comparative	superlative
willingly		
close		
sincerely		
low		

B Use the comparative form of these adverbs in sentences of your own.

1 privately _____

_____

2 nervously _____

_____

3 often _____

_____

C Use the superlative form of these adverbs in sentences of your own.

1 convincingly _____

_____

2 well _____

_____

3 fast _____

_____

91 | Adverbial phrases and clauses

A Improve these sentences by adding adverbial phrases.

1 We crept into the garden _____

_____

2 The tiger moved _____

_____

3 The boy whistled _____

_____

B Improve these sentences by adding adverbial clauses.

1 You can go out _____

_____

2 She cried _____

_____

3 The flowers died _____

_____

SENTENCES

Focus

In *Learning Targets: Grammar and Punctuation Key Stage* 1 the children were introduced to basic sentence punctuation, the idea that a sentence must make sense, and sentences which contain direct speech.

Section 1 of this book revises and reinforces the work in Key Stage 1 and introduces children to indirect speech.

This section deals with the construction of sentences, from simple to complex, recapping on the use of clauses and introducing the idea of the main clause, subject, object and predicate.

Contents

Unit 1: Subject, object and predicate

Unit 2: Clauses

Unit 3: Compound and complex sentences

Assessment

At the end of this section children should be able to:

1   identify the subject, object and predicate of a sentence

2   identify and construct simple sentences

3   identify and construct compound sentences

4   identify and construct complex sentences.

The assessment copymaster is on page 164.

Copymaster 100 A writing task gives the children writing starting points. Explain that you will be looking at their work specifically for sentence construction so they should check carefully to see that they have not used only simple sentences in their work.

Subject, object and predicate

Learning targets

On completion of this unit the children should be able to:

1 ➤➤ identify the subject and object of a sentence

2 ➤➤ identify the predicate of a sentence.

Before you start

Background knowledge

This unit deals with subject, object and predicate in relation to how sentences are constructed. Although not specifically mentioned in the National Literacy Strategy, it is necessary for the children to be comfortable with these concepts within the context of simple sentences before moving on to more sophisticated work with compound and complex sentences.

Resources for Session 1

Copymaster 92 Subject and objects

Copymaster 93 Writing sentences

Resources for Session 2

Copymaster 94 Subjects and predicates

Copymaster 95 Improving sentences

Assessment indicators

- Can the children identify the subject and object within a simple sentence?
- Can they identify the predicate of a sentence?
- Can they expand simple sentences by adding descriptive words to subject and object?

Teaching the sessions

Session 1 ①

Introduction | 20-30 min |

▦ Begin by asking the children what they understand by the term 'sentence'. A sentence must:

- start with a capital letter and end with a full stop/question mark/exclamation mark
- have a verb
- make sense.

Write the following simple sentence on the board:

The girl tore a book.

Explain that every sentence has to have a subject. In an active sentence the subject tells us who or what is doing something. In the sentence above it is the 'girl' who tore the book. In passive sentences the subject tells us who or what is having something done to it, e.g. The book was torn by the girl. In active sentences the object tells us who or what is having something done to it. In this sentence the object is the 'book' which has been torn.

Write some more simple sentences on the board and ask the children to identify the subject and object, e.g.

The dog chased the cat.

The boy broke the window.

The ball landed in the puddle.

Subjects and objects | 20 min |

♣ Give each group **Copymaster 92 Subjects and objects**. Completing sentences in this way reinforces the idea of subject and object. Encourage the children to think of interesting subjects and objects, not just the most obvious. They can make sentences as humorous or unusual as they like.

Summary | 10 min |

▦ Compare the way each group has completed the sentences through class discussion. Can the children work out the relationship between:

- the subject and the verb?
- the object and the verb?

150

Writing sentences 20min

 Copymaster 93 Writing sentences gives the children a list of subject and object pairs from which they must construct simple sentences.

Homework

The children can write five sentences of their own, They should underline the subject and circle the object in each sentence.

Session 2 ②

Introduction 20-30min

Recap on subjects and objects from Session 1.

Write the following sentence on the board and ask the children to identify the subject and object.

   (subject)   (object)

<u>My sister</u> rode <u>her bicycle</u> to school.

Explain that there is a name for all the other words in a sentence except the subject. We call this the 'predicate'. The predicate contains the verb and the object, everything but the subject.

We would divide the same sentence like this:

   (subject) (predicate)

<u>My sister</u> <u>rode her bicycle to school</u>.

Write some more sentences on the board and ask the children to identify the subject and predicate, e.g.

The milkman delivered the milk.

The horse galloped across the field.

Five baby birds hatched in the nest.

Explain to the children that both the subject and the predicate can be made more interesting by adding descriptive words, e.g.

  (subject)   (predicate)

<u>My older sister</u> <u>rode to school on her new mountain bicycle</u>.

Go back to the sentences on the board where the children have identified the subject and predicate. Can they add to the sentences to make them more interesting?

This is a good opportunity to look at the confused usage of 'I' and 'me'. Explain that 'I' is always used as the subject of a sentence, e.g.

  (subject)   (predicate)

<u>I</u> <u>went for a walk</u>.

<u>Tom and I</u> <u>went swimming</u>.

'Me' is always used in the predicate, e.g.

  (subject)   (predicate)

<u>Dad</u> <u>is buying me a new jacket</u>.

Subjects and predicates 20-25min

Give each group **Copymaster 94 Subjects and predicates**. In Section A, the children must identify the subjects and predicates. Remind them to look for the subject first, then the rest is the predicate. In Section B, they must complete the sentences by adding interesting predicates.

Summary 10min

Compare answers through class discussion.

Improving sentences 20min

Give each child **Copymaster 95 improving sentences**. Section A requires the children to identify the subject and improve the sentences by adding to it. Section B requires the children to identify the predicate and improve the sentence by adding to it.

92 | Subjects and objects

A Complete these sentences by adding a subject to each one.

1 [   ] swung down from the trees.

2 [   ] crashed into the barrier.

3 [   ] makes magic spells.

4 [   ] wants to be an astronaut.

B Complete these sentences by adding an object to each one.

1 The angry man shouted at [   ] .

2 My Aunt Maud bought a [   ] .

3 Tasmin rides a [   ] .

4 The clown threw a [   ] .

Writing sentences

Use these pairs of subjects and objects in sentences of your own.

1 subject = the donkey
object = the sand

_____

_____

2 subject = my brother
object = leg

_____

_____

3 subject = the gate
object = my finger

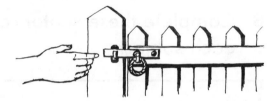

_____

_____

4 subject = the river
object = our house

_____

_____

5 subject = the policeman
object = the boy

_____

_____

94 | Subjects and predicates

A Put a ring around the subject and underline the predicate in each sentence.

1 I did my homework on the computer.

2 The rain lasted for three days.

3 Harry has broken his wrist.

4 My pet tortoise got lost in the garden.

5 The lighthouse stood on the edge of the cliff.

B Complete these sentences by adding an interesting predicate to each subject.

1 The ghost _____

_____

2 My friend Oliver _____

_____

3 The cottage _____

_____

4 Our house _____

_____

5 Sonia and I _____

_____

Improving sentences

A Underline the subject in these sentences.

Rewrite each sentence, making the subject more interesting.

1 The book lay on the floor.

_____

2 These shoes need cleaning.

_____

3 The singer sang my favourite song.

_____

4 Birds have nested in the oak tree.

_____

B Underline the predicate in these sentences.

Rewrite each sentence, making the predicate more interesting.

1 The lake was at the edge of the wood.

_____

2 Frank walked down the road.

_____

3 Tracey went to the park.

_____

4 I switched on the computer.

_____

UNIT 2 | Clauses

Learning target

On completion of this unit the children should be able to:

1 ➤➤ understand clauses through
- identifying the main clause in a long sentence (Y5T3)
- investigating sentences which contain more than one clause (Y5T3)
- investigating how clauses are connected. (Y5T3)

Before you start

Background knowledge

This unit should be tackled before Adjectives Unit 7 and Adverbs Unit 9, to introduce the idea of clauses. All sentences have a main clause which can be a sentence in itself. Other clauses in sentences, such as adjectival and adverbial clauses, are known as subordinate clauses. These cannot stand alone and make sense.

Resources for Session 1

Copymaster 96 Clauses

Copymaster 97 Using clauses

Assessment indicators

- Can the children identify the main clause in a sentence?
- Can the children identify the 'second' clause in a sentence?
- Can they improve writing by using sentences with more than one clause?

Teaching the session

Session 1 ①

Introduction 20-30 min

▨ Introduce the children to the term 'clause' as a group of words which has a verb but is not a sentence.

Write the following on the board:

because he broke his leg

Ask the children to:

- identify the verb
- say why it is not a sentence.

Repeat the activity several times, e.g.

and fell over

but I can't find it

when I go to sleep

Explain to the children that

- sentences are made up of clauses
- every sentence has a main clause
- some sentences have a main clause and other clauses
- the main clause is the only type of clause that can be a sentence in itself.

Write some examples of main clause sentences on the board, e.g.

We went down to the river.

The banana wasn't ripe.

Explain that adding other clauses to a sentence gives us more information, i.e.

We went down to the river after it had stopped raining.

Main clause = We went down to the river
Second clause = after it had stopped raining

The plant wasn't dead although I forgot to water it.

Main clause = The plant wasn't dead

Second clause = although I forgot to water it

Point out how a comma is often used in sentences where the second clause comes first, i.e.

After it had stopped raining, we went down to the river.

Although I forgot to water it, the plant wasn't dead.

Write some main clause sentences on the board and ask the children to suggest second clauses that could be added to give more information.

The bucket was leaking.

A tile fell off the roof.

I have to make the tea.

Ask the children to reverse the clauses in each sentence and to add punctuation.

Clauses
[20 min]

Children will need plenty of practice in identifying main and second clauses in sentences. **Copymaster 96 Clauses** should be tackled as a group activity, with you on hand for support.

Summary
[10 min]

Compare answers through class discussion. If any of the groups have wrongly identified main clauses, write the clause on the board and ask the children if it is a sentence on its own, e.g.

and we go swimming

if I get to school early

Writing
[20-25 min]

Copymaster 97 Using clauses, Section A, gives the children the opportunity to expand main clause sentences with second clauses to add more information. Section B requires the children to add main clauses to the second clauses provided in order to make complete sentences.

Homework

The children should find two examples of:

- main clause sentences
- main and second clause sentences in their current reading book.

They can copy the examples, underlining main clauses in red and second clauses in blue.

Underline the main clause in each sentence in red.
Underline the second clause in each sentence in blue.

1 After meeting my friends on Saturday mornings, we go swimming.

2 If I get to school early, I can go on the computer.

3 The bus was late so I didn't get there in time.

4 Although I like it, I don't want pizza today.

5 He always does his homework before he watches television.

6 The tiger prowled around before he settled down to sleep.

7 The people queued even though they knew there were no tickets left.

8 I play tennis whenever I have the chance.

A Copy these main clause sentences and add a second clause to make them more interesting.
You can put the second clause before or after the main clause.

1 The lake was frozen.

_____

_____

2 Birds nest in that tree.

_____

_____

3 These shoes are too tight.

_____

_____

B Add a main clause to each of these second clauses to complete the sentences.
You can put the main clause before or after the second clause.

1 if you lose that watch

_____

_____

2 although I enjoyed it

_____

_____

3 when it's five o'clock

_____

_____

UNIT 3

Compound and complex sentences

Learning targets

On completion of this unit the children should be able to:

1 ➡➡ secure control of compound sentences (Y6T3)

2 ➡➡ secure control of complex sentences. (Y6T3)

Before you start

Background knowledge

The National Literacy Strategy refers to 'complex' sentences and this has been taken to mean any type of sentence other than the simple sentence made up of a single main clause. The term 'complex' sentences, therefore, covers compound sentences and complex sentences.

Compound sentences are made up of two or more simple sentences joined by 'and', 'but' or 'or'.

Complex sentences are made up of two or more clauses which are not of equal importance. In a complex sentence there is one main clause, with other clauses joined by any one of the pronouns or conjunctions given in the chart that follows.

Pronouns	Conjunctions		
who	before	although	as
which	when	whenever	after
whose	until	unless	so
	where	because	if
	while	even though	

Resource for Session 1

Copymaster 98 Making compound sentences

Resource for Session 2

Copymaster 99 Making complex sentences

Assessment indicators

- Can the children identify compound sentences?
- Can they use compound sentences in their writing?
- Can they identify complex sentences?
- Can they use complex sentences in their writing?

Teaching the sessions

Session 1 ❶

Introduction 20-30 min

▦ Recap on the work the children have done on main clauses, reminding them that every sentence has a main clause. A simple sentence is made up of one main clause.

Explain to the children that you are going to investigate compound sentences. These are sentences which are made up of two simple sentences joined by 'and', 'but' or 'or'.

Write the following simple sentences on the board:

The town was crowded.

I like this book.

I might go swimming.

Ask the children to change these simple sentences into compound sentences, e.g.

The town was crowded and I felt very tired when I got home.

I like this book but I don't like this one.

I might go swimming or I might go to the park.

Ask the children to identify the main clause in each sentence.

Ask them to identify the second clause and ensure they understand that they need to include the conjunction.

Repeat this activity, asking the children to suggest simple sentences and then turn them into compound sentences.

Making compound sentences   `20min`

♣ **Copymaster 98 Making compound sentences** reinforces the use of the three conjunctions in forming compound sentences.

Summary   `10-15 min`

▦ Compare the completed sentences through class discussion. Write some of the children's suggestions on the board and investigate:

- the two simple sentences each compound sentence is made up of
- the main clause in each compound sentence
- the second clause in each compound sentence.

Ensure the children include the conjunction in the second clause.

Using compound sentences   `20-30min`

👤 Ask the children to choose one of the following titles:

My Hobby
My Pet
My Bedroom

They should write at least 10 lines on the subject they have chosen, including at least three compound sentences. Encourage the children to work in draft and be on hand to help them spot simple sentences that they can join to make compound sentences.

Homework

The children can make a final copy of their work and underline the compound sentences they have used.

Session 2   ②

Introduction   `20-30min`

▦ Recap on the work the children have done in Session 1 on compound sentences.

Explain to the children that you are now going to investigate complex sentences. These are sentences which are made up of two or more clauses which are not of equal importance. The main clause and the second clause can be joined by:

- the pronouns 'who', 'which' or 'whose'

- a variety of conjunctions but not 'and', 'but' or 'or'.

Ask the children to suggest other conjunctions they could use and list them on the board.

Write the following simple sentences on the board from Session 1:

The town was crowded.

I like this book.

I might go swimming.

Ask the children to change these simple sentences into complex sentences, using the pronouns or conjunctions from their list, e.g.

The town was crowded so I went home.

I like this book even though it is about spiders.

I might go swimming after school today.

Ask the children to identify the main clause in each sentence. Ask them to identify the second clause and ensure they understand the need to include the conjunction.

Repeat the activity, asking the children to suggest simple sentences and then turn them into complex sentences.

Making complex sentences   `20min`

♣ **Copymaster 99 Making complex sentences** reinforces the use of conjunctions and pronouns in forming compound sentences.

Summary   `10-15 min`

▦ Compare the completed sentences through class discussion. Write some of the children's suggestions on the board and investigate:

- the main clause in each complex sentence
- the second clause in each complex sentence

Ensure the children include the conjunction/pronoun in the second clause.

Using complex sentences   `20-30min`

👤 Give the children their work on:
My Hobby

My Pet

My Bedroom

from Session 1.

Ask them to edit their work so that they include complex sentences as well as three compound sentences. They can add more if they wish. Encourage them to work in draft at this stage.

Homework

The children can make a final copy of their work and underline the complex sentences they have used.

161

Making compound sentences

Complete each of these sentences in the three different ways with

and...

but...

or...

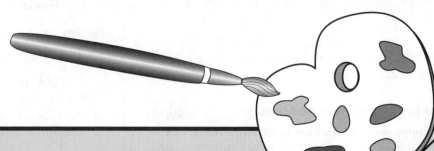

1 We could ring Masie today and _____

_____

We could ring Masie today but _____

_____

We could ring Masie today or _____

_____

2 The weather forecaster says it might rain today and

_____

The weather forecaster says it might rain today but

_____

The weather forecaster says it might rain today or

_____

3 I would like to have a puppy and_____

_____

I would like to have a puppy but _____

_____

I would like to have a puppy or _____

_____

Use a different conjunction from the box to complete these complex sentences.

| after before although |
| while so |

1 I am going to visit Uncle John _____

_____

2 You must take these books back to the library _____

_____

3 The car has broken down _____

_____

4 She telephoned her friend _____

_____

5 He posted the letter yesterday _____

_____

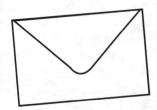

Choose one of these as a starting point for a story:

Imagine you are going to visit a cousin whom you have never met before.

Write a short story which opens with the sentence:
I had never been so surprised in all my life!

Write a short story with the title 'My Birthday'.

Write a story about a group of animals which are threatened by the building of a new road.

Write a story which has the following:
a storm
a rescue